IRAN

A COMPREHENSIVE STUDY OF SOCIO-ECONOMIC CONDITION

Z. HEYAT

Library of Congress Catalog Card No.:

83-080460

Eastern Publishing Society

INTRODUCTION

This book embodies elements of research and a comprehensive study on Socio-Economic conditions of Iran with emphasis on economic development during Pahlavi dynasty. It deals with important, yet controversial issues related to different phases of Iran's struggle to surpass backwardness. It dwells on the problems which confronted the Iranian ruling class to achieve the ultimate goal, as promised by the late Shah of Iran, THE GREAT CIVILIZATION.

Dr. Heyat, the author, presents a true picture of Iran's five development plans and their consequences on the Iranian society.

He has written numerous books and many publications on economy and finance used as text books and incorporated into the curriculum of Iran's Universities and higher educational systems.

During his professorship at the University of Tehran School of Economy and Management, School of Trade, and the Center for International Research and Studies, he has accomplished an active role in public service, and has served his country with great integrity as Managing Director of Banks, Secretary General of Banks Syndicate (Kanoon Bankha) and finally Under Secretary of the Ministry of Trade.

Dr. Heyat holds a doctorate degree in Economy from the University of Paris. He has also obtained a Phd. from the prestigious London School of Economy in International Economy and Expansion of the Economy of the Third World Nations.

It is with utmost pleasure to introduce this collection which explores new methods in achieving a better understanding with hope to rectify the structure of past and present Socio-Economic condition of Iran.

Amir Nejat

P R E F A C E

The main purpose of this book is to present a program for reconstruction and development of Iran without excessive dependence on foreign elements.

Towards this goal, it is necessary to transform the existing dualism of socio-economics to a homogenous society, in which the well being of all people is provided and secured.

In different chapters of this book, I have focused on the following:

Economic conditions of Iran in the past centuries before the Pahlavi dynasty, economic changes and it's progress during the Pahlavi regime, social conditions and changes in the working class, women, and other group conditions, shortcomings and weaknesses of Iran's economic development, the Iranian revolution of 1978 and its effects, principle ideas necessary for a political, social, as well as economic system, democracy and its conditions, general characteristics of a welfare economic program and proposals for various sectors of the economy, and the political framework for implementing a welfare program, considered to be democratic.

After many years of teaching in various Iranian universities, and extensive services in the private sector of the economy, particularly in regard to underdeveloped countries, it is my intention to present a program in conformity with the present requirements of the country.

Dr. Z. Heyat

California, U.S.A.
January 1983

TABLE OF CONTENTS

REFERENCES

IRAN DICTATORSHIP AND DEVELOPMENT	Fred Haliday	1980
ECONOMIC DEVELOPMENT OF IRAN	The World Bank	1974
DEVELOPMENT DIALOGUE	I.F.D.A.	1981
THIRD WORLD	Sanirami Quarterly Journal	1979
SMALL IS BEAUTIFUL	Schumacher	1975
SIX GREAT IDEAS	Mortimor J. Adler	1981
ECONOMY, ECOLOGY ETHICS	Herman E. Daly	1980
REDISTRIBUTION WITH GROWTH	The World Bank	1976
GOVERNMENT BY THE PEOPLE	James Macgreger	1975
CREATING ALTERNATIVE FUTURE	Hazel Henderson	1978
IRAN-THE ILLUSION OF POWER	Robert Graham	1979
HUMAN RIGHTS	United Nations	1948
IRAN'S ENERGY IN THE FUTURE	D. Firidoon Fescharaki	1981
IRAN'S REVOLUTION AND THE ROLE OF SCIENCE	Dr. Ali Bechaghi	1980
IRAN IN THRESHOLD OF DESTINY		1980
WORLD WIDE INFLATION	Dr. Z. Heyat	1977
INTERNATIONAL TRADE - SECOND VOLUME	Dr. Z. Heyat	1975
THE ANNUAL REPORTS OF BANK MARKAZI OF IRAN		1960/1981

INTERVIEWS: Engineer Bazerghan, Banisadr, General Madani and others

IRAN

CHAPTER 1

A BRIEF STUDY OF ECONOMIC CONDITIONS OF IRAN BEFORE PAHLAVI DYNASTY

In ancient times, Iran held an important economic and commerce position among the world's major powers. She maintained commercial relations not only with her neighbors, but on a global bases. During the past centuries, Iran's domestic economic and foreign conditions had been influenced by her trading events experiencing much flucuation.

During the periods of having powerful and efficient government and consequently enjoying internal and external security, agriculture industry and foreign trade progressed to a great extent.

During other periods, as a result of foreign wars and internal disorders, the economic and international trade of the country declined. For example, agriculture industry and foreign trade deteriorated with the invasion of Mongul and during their reign in Iran.

During Safavy dynasty, particularly during the reign of Shah Abbas The Great, with increasing power of central government, construction of roads, special attachment of Safavy Kings toward the welfare of the people, and economic-development was revitalized and made major progress. Agricultural and industrial products were, not only sufficient to meet domestic needs, but ample enough to export to other countries. During this period, Iranian exports comprised a variety of products, namely industrial output; silk, velvet textiles, and handicrafts. There was no need at this time to import much foreign goods, which consisted of spices, perfumes, and coffee. All other domestic needs were produced internally. Usually, export and import of the country were in balance.

In short, we can conclude that, until the 18th century, among other nations of the world, Iran was the nation that produced it's own needs with such a high caliber of quality that she created a strong market for her products. Her textile industry, for example, attained such excellent position that the government of Britain, in order to protect its own textile industry, banned the import of Iranian textile. This shows the importance of Iranian industrial products at that time.

From the beginning of the 19th century, when the industrial revolution had made great progress, first in England, and later in other European countries; the industrial products of those countries gradually entered the Iranian market and her domestic products met with intense competition. Furthermore, because of perpetual internal disturbances, conflicts, instability, weakness of government, industry, agriculture and commerce were neglected. As a result, the country was impoverished and remained backward. Competition of foreign machine made products coupled with the political backing of great powers, namely, Britain and Russia, their interference in Iran's internal affairs, due to their imported products, had deplorable effects in Iran's economy and trade.

At the beginning of the 19th century, after the defeat of Iran in the war by Russia, treaties and commercial agreements were imposed by that country on Iran that resulted in the domination of Iran by the colonial powers and deprived Iran of being capable of defending herself against foreign domination.

The first treaty that limited Iran's power to levy custom duties independently to its imports was imposed by Russia through the Treaty Of Gaolestan, which concluded in October 1813, and later, the Treaty Of Tourkomanschay in February 1828, after the defeat of Iran in the wars between Iran and Russia.

According to those treaties, all kinds of Russian products could be imported to Iran without any limitations and Iran had the right only to impose upon them a maximum amount of five percent duty. Later, after the establishment of capitulation in Iran, England and some other countries concluded commercial agreements with Iran; and by including the most favored clause in their agreements, they benefited from the same advantages that Russia had acquired through the above mentioned treaties. These treaties and commercial agreements tied the hands of Iran from acting freely and destroyed Iran's economic independence. As a result, machine made products of European countries defeated Iran's domestic industries and the market of the country fell in the hands of foreigners.

A Frenchman named Ogen Flander, who, in 1842 on a French mission, came in company to the court of Mohammadshah, explained in his diary, the condition of Kashans industries, (Kashan, a city in the central part of Iran). His observations are a good example that show the deplorable condition of industries of Iran in that period and the early effects of foreign competition with domestic products. Ogen Flander's observations are as follows:

> "Kashan has many factories that produce printed textiles and satins of strong and elegant quality, with many factories of velvet and kashmir scarfs. But the imports from England that began thirty years before and is increasing every year has deplorable effects on Kashan factories. Although, some of the factories are working; every day some of them are closing; and one becomes full of sadness seeing that most of the factories are standing still. During Safavy dynasty, this city was the first industrial city of Iran; but at the present, nothing is in existence like two centuries before when factories had more than three thousand workers."

During this time, contrary to the previous times, the exports of Iran with the exception of carpet, consisted of raw materials and agricultural products. Due to bad packing and grading, those products were sold below international prices. Imports of Iran consisted of all kinds of consumer goods. The main imports were cotton, textile, sugar and tea. In some years, textile was more than forty percent of the total imports. Foreign trade of Iran in this period was always insufficient, the deficit was growing every year, and the balance was paid by exporting gold.

In Summary, we can conclude that: Iran at the end of the 19th century became an agricultural country without any industry. Her central government was very weak. During the 19th century, Kings of Kaghar, by according extraordinary concessions to governments of Russia and Britain had put the country under their political and economic domination and thereby the country no longer enjoyed complete political and economic independence.

In 1891, the first movement in Iran against foreign domination took shape in protest from the part of religious leaders and merchants against granting the monopoly of tobacco to an English company. Gradually the protests increased and resulted in a constitutional revolution.

This constitutional revolution that occurred during the years of 1901-1905 was an attempt by intellectuals and merchants to reform the kingdom and establish a parlimentary government. There is much discussion and different ideas about the factors that created this revolution. What is important, is that this revolution was the first attempt from the people of Iran to limit the power of Kings and transfer the power of legislation to elected representatives of the people.

Unfortunately, this action provided no essential change in governing the country. Although there was a parliment, the old power groups again had the power in their hands because, at that time, other groups were also weak.

CHAPTER 2

ECONOMIC DEVELOPMENT OF IRAN UNDER REZA SHAH PAHLAVI

During the first world war, British, Russian, as well as Turkish forces invaded Iran, and the country was greatly ruined. At the end of the war; as a result of communist Revolution in Russia; Quagar King's main support had vanished. Furthermore, there came great changes in conditions of the world and also inside Iran, that facilitated the Iranian government's intervention to improve the economic and trade conditions of the country; as abolition of the concessions and limitations that was imposed by the Tsarist government of Russia in the past. At the end of the war in 1919, there was no central government of any adequate kind in Iran, and separatist movements were in power in the provinces of Khosistan, Gilan and Khorasan. The only coherent Iranian force at the center was the military unit named Cossak established by Russian officers in 1879. The leader of this force of 3000 men, with British encouragement, staged a bloodless coup on February 1921.

Reza Khan, the leader of the coup, first became minister of war, and later prime minister. Within a short time, he established himself as the dominant personality in the country, and was able to maintain order and security in the country. The people of Iran who were tired of continual insecurity, disorder and chaos did not oppose him, but supported him. In 1925, the Quagar dynasty was disposed of by approval of parliment and Reza Khan became King; and so a new dynasty named Pahlavi was founded.

Reza Khan after becoming king, established the first centralized government in Iran. He built a modern army to enforce government control over the whole country. Consequently, all separatist movements were crushed. He established the first ministerial system in Iran, developed an educational, health and transport system that was before non-existent in Iran. He also began to encourage a small industrialization program in the country. Reza Shah, from the very beginning of his reign made great efforts to secure political, economic, foreign trade, and the monetary independence for Iran; such as abolition of the colonial treaties and capitulation; establishment of the National Bank Of Iran and granting it the monopoly of bank notes; and the creation and construction of roads and railways.

Establishment of the first independent custom duties regulations-

After more than one century of limitations, in the third day of April 23, 1928, the first independent custom duty law was approved by the Iranian parliment as the first step in procuring economic independence of the country. As a result of this law, the regulations of the Tourkmanchay treaty and other contracts unfavorable to Iran's interests were abolished. In this law of custom duties, the tariff of import duties was very low; in order to encourage the other countries to conclude commercial agreements with Iran; and so, it had no protective clauses. Most trading partners of Iran concluded commercial agreements with her. Terms of the agreements were for eight years.

Approval of the law of monopoly of foreign trade of Iran-

In spite of the important successes and improvements that occurred during the years 1925-1929 in Iran's economy and commerce, the world's great economic depression in 1930 had unfavorable effects on Iran's economy and commerce. Consequently, the foreign trade of Iran dropped. Prices of Iranian export that mostly consisted of agricultural products and raw materials decreased immensly and as a result of lowering the prices of manufactured goods, the imports of those goods increased and the newly established industries of Iran were faced with difficulties. At this time, Iran's newly established industries needed protection; but as mentioned before, the tariff of custom duties of 1928 was very low and because the term of the custom duty agreements concluded with other countries was to expire in 1936, the government was unable to benefit from this custom duty policy to protect domestic industries until 1936.

The government of Iran, in order to neutralize the unfavorable effects of the world depression and protect it's industries and also provide necessary funds to import capital goods, regulated the law of monopoly of foreign trade that was approved by Majliss on the 6th of March in 1930, and put it into action immediately.

According to this law and subsequent complimentary laws and their amendments; import and export of all goods was in the hands of the government. Undoubtedly, the government did not intend for the above law to monopolize all imports and exports. This procedure was in contrast with the Iranian economic regime that advocated the free enterprise system; and also, the government at this time was not prepared to handle such an enormous monopoly. In fact, the monopoly law was a law of the quota system and control of foreign trade, as follows:

> "At the beginning of every year, the government fixed the quantity of each good that was permitted to be imported by taking into account the domestic demand and quantity produced at home and only giving import permits to private traders to the extent of that quantity, and in the following year would lower the quota as much as the production of that good was increased. Exports, with the exception of those goods that government intended to handle directly or assign to other institutions were freely

exported by private traders."

According to the monopoly law of foreign trade, the import of foreign consumer goods was dependent on the export of the same amount of Iranian goods. But the import of capital goods and machine tools necessary for industries was exempt from this condition. The enforcement of the above law naturally resulted in the lowering of imports and the increasing of exports and the balancing of foreign trade.

The law of exchange control-

In order to protect the value of the country's money, exchange control was introduced and the buying and selling of foreign exchange was assigned to a special commission called the "Exchange Commission".

In 1932, as great oscillations occurred in the price of silver in world markets, the government of Iran changed the cover of Iranian money from silver to gold; and purchased the right of printing and the circulation of bank notes from the British Imperial Bank, and gave it in 1933 to the Iranian National Bank (Bank Mellie Iran) and by doing this, the government acquired for the first time an independent monetary policy.

From the year 1931, after implementing the monopoly law of foreign trade and exchange control regulations, the government began to intervene effectively in different sectors of the economy of the country, and took necessary steps; for introducing new industries and protecting them; limiting the imports and developing exports; and balancing the foreign trade. Consequently, as a result of creating a much favorable economic environment, and pursuing wise and suitable exchange in monetary and trade policies, a considerable number of imports replacing industries were established in the country. Even Reza Shah, at the later years of his reign, intended to establish a steel industry in Iran and so doing, he imported the necessary machine tools. Unfortunately, because of World War II, he was unable to achieve his wish.

During the reign of Reza Shah, parallel to the development of Iran's foreign trade ,industries, after long periods of deficit, which resulted in 1941 in a surplus of foreign trade, economic conditions were so favorable that it promised the prospect of a healthy and successful development in the years to come.

Reza Shah, during the short 16 year period of

his reign, made great efforts for improving the economic, political and administrative culture of the country (of which we only mentioned briefly some important ones in the economic field). He introduced a new system of education and health previously non-existent in Iran. For the first time, he established a university in Tehran, and also sent every year, hundreds of students to Europe to study and specialize in engineering, medicine and other fields of science. He also made great efforts for the liberation and freedom of women and their education. Achievements and actions of Reza Shah to some extent, are comparable with the actions of Ataturk, the leader of Turkey.

In comparison to Ataturk, Reza Shah, undoubtedly succeeded to awaken Iran from centuries of ignorance and backwardness and create a favorable environment and necessary infrastructure for future advancement. Neverthless, he had two important shortcomings. Reza Shah was very greedy and by using his influence, he acquired thousands of villages and properties and great amounts of cash in foreign and domestic banks. His actions were imitated by his family, his court, and high civil and military officials of government. Ataturk during his life had no inclination to accumulate personal wealth and when he died, he left only one bed, and a desk.

Ataturk organized a political party with a national ideology that survived even after his death, but Reza Shah governed the country like ancient Kings of Iran, with despotism and absolute power. Every thing was dependent on him personally, so when he was abdicated, there reigned chaos and disorder in the country for a long time.

CHAPTER 3

ECONOMIC CONDITIONS OF IRAN DURING THE SECOND WORLD WAR

On August 25, 1941, Iran was occupied by Russian, English, and American powers. Reza Shah was abdicated by the decision of the occupying powers, and his son, Mohammad Reza, was appointed in his place as King of Iran. The existence of the occupying powers in Iran had unfavorable effects on all aspects of the economic and political life of the country.

In order to meet the needs of the foreign powers, enormous amount of bank notes were printed and put into circulation. Also, as a result of war, agricultural and industrial production was depressed and volumes of imports decreased. Consequently, prices increased rapidly more than 70%, and intense inflation spread in the country.

As a result of the weakening power of Iran's central government, it was not possible to implement the law of monopoly of foreign trade and exchange control. Consequently, volumes of export decreased and because of increasing the prices of imports, the value of imports increased; (although its volume decreased) and thereby again, a large disequilibrium appeared in the foreign trade of the country.

During wartime, newspapers and all other kinds of press became free in Iran, and workers organized unions and many political parties were formed. At the end of the war, two independent governments by support of the Russian army were created; one in Kordistan and the other in Azarbaydjan. After the war, the central government with the support of the United States Of America and the United Nations, extended it's control to those areas again. The Toudeh party that was formed during wartime and had developed rapidly, supported the separationist government of Azarbaydjan and Kordistan and also was an unquestionable follower of Russian policy in Iran. Because of this policy, the Toudeh party lost much of its reputation and importance after the second world war.

Most of the advanced countries of the world (capitalist or socialist), in order to remedy the unfavorable effects of war and inflation on their economy, established controls for import, export, and foreign exchange of their country; thereby most of them succeeded in two or three years to remove the effects of war and brought the economy to a normal condition.

After the occupying powers left Iran, the monopoly law of foreign trade and the law of exchange control was formally valid, but the government followed the free trade policy. Consequently, imports of nonessential consumer goods increased and exports decreased and foreign trade became a large deficit. The value of Irans exports before the war equaled the value of its imports. Consequently in 1949, only one fifth of the value of imports, and payment for the remaining four fifths of the imports were financed by Iran's oil income. During this period, the government of Iran acquired enormous amounts of foreign exchange from oil and other sources, but instead of using those funds to develop the economy, they were used to import nonessential consumer goods; because the government was of the opinion that opening the doors for foreign trade would remove inflation. This unwise policy was not effective in combatting the inflation, it only imbalanced foreign trade to such an extent that its improvements did not seem possible in the forseeable future.

CHAPTER 4

IRAN'S ECONOMIC DEVELOPMENT PLANS

After the second world war, in the year 1945, the government of Iran, in order to develop the economy of the country, devised a plan to create a special institution called "plan organization" and appointed a board to run it. The board prepared a plan comprising of some projects that were not coherent or comprehensive, to the sum of 62 billion rials; and at that time, this sum of money exceeded the financial possibility of the country, so the government asked the International Bank for a loan. As per the recommendation of that bank, Morisson Knudson Company, and later the Council of Overseas Consultants (both American firms) studied the plan and reduced it to 21 billion rials.

The first plan called the "first seven year plan", consisted only of some non-coherent projects mostly related to agriculture. The first year of the plan was spent creating the administrative organ of the plan and the implementation of projects began in the second year; but after a short time, because of the nationalization of the oil industry and it's effect on the oil export, the execution of the plan was stopped.

Nationalization of oil and its effects on the economy of Iran-

In March 1951, under the leadership of Dr. Mossadegh, and the proposal of the National Front group in parliment, the oil industry was nationalized and Dr. Mossadegh was chosen by parliment as prime minister to carry out the nationalization program. Because of the opposition of the British government and the "Oil Cartel", Iran did not succeed to sell it's oil; and as the most important source of Iran's exchange income, the country was faced with a great foreign exchange shortage. Consequently, rates of foreign monies increased sharply and the balance of payments became deficitaire. The government in order to remedy this situation passed regulations to limit imports and encourage exports. The basis of the above regulations was the Decree of Council of Ministers dated January 15, 1952. According to this decree, imports and exports were divided into two groups, as follows: essential and nonessential imports; exports needing encouragements, and those not needing it. The exchange income resulting from the export of quality goods in demand in foreign markets was assigned to imports of essential goods and the exchange income of exports not in good demand was allocated to the import of nonessential goods. Furthermore, through concluding clearing and barter agreements with socialist countries, the volume of exports increased and imports decreased.

Despite the above mentioned useful regulations, a large deficit in foreign trade occurred and nearly the whole exchange reserve of the country was exhausted, so that the rate of the dollar rose from 32 rials to 124 rials. The government had not forseen their oil income stopping therefore it had not prepared an alternative non-oil economic program; and the economic conditions of the country deteriorated creating discontent among the people.

At the beginning of 1953, Mossadegh's popularity had decreased and chaos and disorder gradually spread to all parts of the country. Toudeh's party also helped in provoking disorder in the country, trying to penetrate it's influence in all institutions of government, hoping by this method to be able to capture power. The religious leaders especially the Ayatoullah Kashani and Behbahani, who in the first year of Mossadegh's government supported him, began to oppose him and so on the 19th of August, 1953, the Mossadegh government with the help of opposing internal groups and external powers, was put out of power. Mohammad Reza Shah after issuing orders to remove Mossadegh from the premiership, left the country, returned to Iran, and acquired the power of government in his own hands. President Eisenhower of the United States of America and his Secretary of State from Dallas, were hard anti-communists; being convinced that Mossadegh was no more capable to establish order and stability in the country, making political conditions in Iran favorable for the communists to capture power, helped the internal opposition to throw Mossadegh out of power.

Some people exaggerate about the role of Americans in removing Mossadegh from power, but others believe that the deteriorating economic conditions and discontent of the people had a greater role, and they argue that Mossadegh was put out of power by internal forces only, because his followers did not support him any longer.

The Pahlavi regime after August 16, 1953, became stronger than before and Mohammad Reza Shah gradually increased his power and closed all genuine parties and abolished freedom of speech and press and obliged opposition by threatening them through Savak (Secret Police) to be silent or be prosecuted.

The second economic development plan-

The first development plan without being carried out was declared ended in the year 1955. Another plan under the the name of the second year plan was introduced. The amount of this plan was 80 billion rials of which 60% was to be financed from the oil income and 25 billion through foreign loans.

As a result of carrying out this plan, many dams as the dam of Amirkabir and Mohammad Reza Shah were constructed, also, many consumer industries such as sugar factories, textile plants, cement and food processing industries were newly created, or old ones developed. Asphalt roads were built, the railroad from Meshhad to Tehran was completed, and in many important cities of Iran, airports were built. In more than forty towns, pipelines for drinking water were installed.

People of Iran still were not ready to do productive activity on a national level and in the framework of a general plan, and private investment was not sufficient to carry out the projects assigned in the second plan. Therefore, to encourage private investment, the government devalued the rial and benefitted from the gold cover of money, printed extra bank notes, and from those funds, the amount of 7100 million rials were put at the disposal of the private sector to be used in the investment of projects assigned in the plan.

Unfortunately, the above funds were not used in the right ways, and so it created inflation and an imbalanced export economy. The government being short of foreign exchanges, asked for a loan from the International Monetary Fund. The loan was granted and at the same time a program was recommended to be carried out by the government in order to remove inflation, and the foreign exchange deficit. This program called the "Stabilization Program" carried out by the government, was successful in combatting inflation and balancing Iran's payment deficit, but it created a recession and thereby, some of the projects of the second plan were postponed and never carried out.

According to the report of the plan organization, as a result of execution of the second plan, the economy of the country enjoyed 4.3% annual growth. Prices that were increasing moderately in the earlier years of the plan, in the last two years of the plan, increased 10% yearly. At the end of the second plan, agriculture was 31%, industries 12%, services 45% and oil 12% of the national income.

In the year 1962, the government after 14 years experiencing the economic plan, understood that even the best plan in unfavorable social circumstances and infrastructure was doomed to failure. Heavy investments were not producing fruitful results. Therefore, the Shah initiated a program of reforms called the "Revolution of Shah and People", which was formulated with the approval of the people through referendum and put into action. The most important part of the program was land reform, that we will discuss in later chapters. Unfortunately, the land reform program was not carried out correctly, and the result was not as expected. The agriculture of the country was depressed.

The 3rd economic development plan-

In 1962, the third plan that was the most comprehensive in comparison with the previous ones, was formulated for 5½ years. The goals of this plan were: 6% annual growth, a just distribution of income among different groups of people and full employment. In this plan, infrastructure projects enjoyed high priority. Total investment of the third plan was an estimated 230 billion rials, 60% of which was to be financed from oil income, 20% from foreign loans and the remaining 20% from internal sources.

According to statistics published by the plan organization, as a result of implementing the third plan, the country gained a 9% annual growth rate and prices only increased 1.5% yearly.

During this plan, many new dams were built, electric power and communication developed considerably and a trans-country gas pipe line was installed. Also, as a result of the third plan, some heavy industries such as, iron mill and petrochemical industries were created by the government. The private sector also built many new industries such as automobile plants and electronic factories; but most of them only served as assembly plants.

The 4th economic development plan-

In the year 1967, the fourth plan of five years

was put into action. The goals of this plan were fixed as follows: 9.4% annual growth, a just distribution of incomes, decreased dependence on foreign countries in providing essential goods, the making of exports more varied and imporving the efficiency of government services. Total investment for this plan was estimated at 810 billion rials of which 80% was to be financed from the oil income, 8% from foreign loans, and the remainder from internal sources. In this plan, priority was accorded to mechanical industries, petrochemical and other essential industries.

As a result of implementing the fourth plan, mechanical, transport, metal and petrochemical industries developed considerably. The growth rate was 13% more than the government had previously forseen, and per capita income increased to 500 dollars.

The 5th economic development plan-

In the beginning of the year 1973, the fifth plan provided by government was put into action in the amount of 2460 billion rials for five years, and it's amount was alone more that the total sum of the four previous plans.

At first, the growth rate for this plan was fixed at 12½%, but after sharp increases of the oil income from 2 billion dollars to 20 billion dollars at the end of the year, the plan was revised and it's investment sum had doubled to 4636 billion rials. The growth rate was fixed at 26%. In this plan, targets for the growth rate in different sectors were fixed as follows: agriculture 7%, industries and mines 22%, services 16.5%, and oil 51.5%. It was assumed that by carrying out this plan, the share of oil in the national income would increase from 20% to 51% and on the contrary, shares of agriculture would drop from 18% to 8%, industries and mines 22% to 19% and services 40% to 27%.

Because the revised five year plan was very ostentatious and out of proportion with it's physical capabilities and infrastructure facilities of the country, great disequilibrium occurred between the financial and physical resources of the country. As a result; intense inflation spread all over and most of the projects were faced with bottlenecks such as: increased prices of raw materials, great increases of wage and salaries, shortage of skilled man power, shortage of building materials, pressure due to the full capacity of ports and transports, and shortage of electric power.

The above experience proves that money is not sufficient for rapid and sustained growth. Financial resources should always be equal to non-financial resources.

During the fifth year plan, and also in previous years, the slow growth of agriculture caused an increased in food imports (especially meat and dairy) from foreign countries.

In summary, it is concluded, as a result of carrying out the above mentioned development plans, the national income of Iran increased from 200 dollars in 1962 to more than 1500 dollars in 1973 and during this period, the average annual growth rate was more than 10% in comparison to other developing countries.

During the 15 year span of three development plans, the value of agricultural products in fixed prices increased 50%, construction 300%, industries and mines 400%, services 400%, oil 1000%, water and electric 1000% and exports more than 500%. Also during this period, many important roads had been constructed, electric power in towns had been installed, and communications widely developed. In a majority of towns, a pure drinking system was provided and a suitable infrastructure was built that created favorable conditions for future rapid industrialization of the country. During this time, the population of the country increased from 23 million to 35 million and the non rural population grew from 35% to 45%.

The rapid growth in recent years in Iran was first due to the sharp increase of the oil income. Oil being an exhaustible resource is in fact the capital of the country. However, the government had considered it as income, and for this reason, the growth rate inflated. Therefore, the real growth rate was much less than what the government claimed. A great part of the growth besides the oil income was due to the increase of government services that in fact did not produce goods, but only a demand for goods, creating inflation. Agriculture was at the weakest point of Iran's economic development. Consequently, the country became dependent on imports from abroad to feed its people. Most of the private industries were only assembly plants and they were also dependent on raw materials, spare parts and semifinished products from foreign sources.

In recent years, after the oil income increased immensely, rapid growth and ambitious projects created great imbalances in different sectors of the economy and in different areas of the country, and inequality in income groups. The rich became richer and the poor became poorer, and as a result of these imbalances, the economic growth stopped in the year of 1977. Discontentment among the people increased, and an uprising of the people of Iran took place at the end of 1978.

CHAPTER 5

IRAN'S AGRICULTURAL DEVELOPMENT AND LAND REFORM

Before the land reform-

The natural conditions and climate of Iran is not favorable for agriculture. Fifty-five percent of the country's 165 million hectares of total land is uncultivated desert, mountains and swamps; and another thirty percent or more is forest and pasture. Only an estimated twelve percent of total land is suitable for cultivation, and according to traditional farming methods only half of it (8 million hectares) is cultivated at any time. Some officials claim that 20 million hectares are cultivable; but there exists some considerable amount of difficulty in using it. Above all, there exists a water shortage. Some people think it would have been better for the country if Iran had enough water and adequate rainfall instead of oil.

Before the land reform, the basic unit used to measure ownership was a village, or one sixth of a village that is called "Dang". It is estimated that there are 50,000 villages in Iran, each having between 20 to 500 inhabitants.

Table 1 Land ownership before the reform

Type of conversion	% of all land owned	number of villages	% of villages
large proprietors	56.0	13,569	34.43
(those owning more than 100 hectares)	33.8		
small proprietors	10-12	16,522	41.93
royal domain	10-13	812	2.06
religious endowments	1-2	713	1.81
tribal holdings	13.0	-	-
public domain	3-4	1,444	3.67
other holdings	6.15	6,346	16.10

Source: "Iran Dictatorship And Development"
by Fred Halliday

The land owning class as shown in Table 1 was formed in different ways during the previous centuries. It included members of the court who had been given land by Shahs, traditional landowners, tribal leaders and merchants who had bought land out of trading profits. Most of the owners were absent landowners who lived in towns, and were considered to be among the Iranian bourgeois.

The most powerful group of landowners consisted of 400 to 500 families, some of whom owned 300 villages. 37 families alone owned 19,000 villages, which is around 38% of the total villages. Reza Shah appropriated for himself between 1920 and 1930, 2100 villages, making him the largest landowner in the country. Only 5% of the peasants in Iran owned the land that they cultivated.

The agricultural activity was performed in two important ways: the first was through unpaid labor for the benefit of land owners, and the second was through various forms of share-cropping systems. The share-cropping system consisted of farmers working on the land for a pre-determined share of the crop. This system differed from one area to another, but the most common system was for the product to be divided into five areas: land, labor, water, animals and seeds.

The peasants were usually divided into two groups: Possessors of Nassaghdar, those who were permanently entitled to work on a piece of land at 20% of the crop for their work; and temporary laborers called Khoshnishin, who received an even smaller share. Nassaghdar's owned mostly animals, so they were able at times to acquire more that 20% of the crop. Before the land reform, there existed a system of hierarchy in the village, that consisted of landowners, animal owning intermediaries, Nassaghdars, and laborers. This preexisting hierarchy provided the basis of which the land reform took place and to some extent, determined the character of social structure after the land reform.

Although the country shared many problems with other underdeveloped countries in agricultural activities, it had also some specific characteristics. First of all, Iran had never been directly under colonization, therefore, it had never been encouraged to produce export crops. Production met domestic needs, and the only major export was cotton and dried fruits. Another characteristic of Iran's countryside is the absence of peasant revolt in the past, the reason is due to the existence of vast distances between villages and permanent threat of raiding nomads. Therefore, it was concluded that the regime was in no danger from the peasants, so the Shah introduced the land reform in order to transform the countryside economically and socially.

The reform and its various phases:

Land reform in Iran began in 1962 and was comleted officially in 1970. Land reform was the most important item of the Shah's reform plan, because it had great impact on the social structure changes, effecting 50% of the population that was living in the countryside. In 1949, the Shah distributed 517 of his own villages (out of 2100) among cultivators. In general, landlords retained power until the reform program and in 1959, they blocked the land reform bill that had been presented by government to parliment.

In January 1962, after dissolution of parliment, the Shah obtained approval of the people through referendum for this reform program that was called "White Revolution of King and People". The land reform program was decided by the Shah through the encouragement of President Kennedy of the United States, for the purpose of creating equality among peasants and also to integrate agriculture with the general economy of the country. The law that was named the first phase of the land reform contained four main provisions as follows:

1- Ownership of land was limited to one village or six Dangs of separate villages. Orchards, tea plantations, groves and mechanized land were exempted.

2- Land owners were to be compensated over the 15 years on the basis of the taxes they paid previously. Peasants who receive land had to pay the value of the land plus 10% in 15 years.

3- Land was to be distributed to those who were already cultivating land. Those who provided more than labor had priority over those who provided only labor. Nassaghdars and laborers were next in line to receive land. All peasants receiving land had to become members of cooperatives.

4- In villages where distribution did not take place, landlords had no more right to arbitrarily dismiss the farmers. Share-cropping was raised in favor of the peasants; 5% on irrigated land and 10% on non-irrigated land.

At first, this law aroused considerable enthusiasm in the countryside because the peasants hoped that it's execution would enable landlords to lose their control over the land, and all peasants would receive a piece of land. They were disapointed. After implementing the first phase, official figures showed that by October 1972, after a decade of carrying out the first phase, only 30% of the villages were covered; and less than 10% had been distributed. Only one fifth of the peasants benefited from the first phase of land reform. A considerable number of landowners, in order to escape redistribution, transferred their excess land to their relatives. Others carried out token mechanization and drove the peasants off the land in order to keep their lands or change their farms into orchards in order to evade redistribution. Some landowners, by bribing reform officials, were able to retain some of the lands to which they were not entitled.

The second stage of the land reform was implemented in January,1963. It was designed to cover those lands which had not been affected by the first phase. Under the second stage of land reform, landlords had to choose one of the following alternatives:

1- To rent the land to peasants on 30 year leases.
2- To sell the land to peasants at a mutually agreed price.
3- To divide the land in proportion to the prevailing crop sharing system.
4- To establish joint stock companies in which landlords and peasants are to be shareholders.
5- To purchase land from peasants.

Most landlords (about 80%) chosed the second option and reached tenacy agreements with peasants, and as a result of it, a total of 1,246,652 peasant families received leases on the land that they cultivated. The second phase affected more peasant families than the first phase of land reform, but fewer peasants in the second stage acquired land. On the whole, in the first phase of land reform, 700,000 families received land, and 210,000 families received land in the second phase.

The peasants were not satisfied with the lease system so they did not try to improve productivity and thereby, agricultural production decreased.

In 1968, the third phase of land reform was introduced that was intended to convert tenancy agreements of phase two onto ownership. As a result of carrying out the third stage, about 738,000 families acquired land. Althogether in the three phases of land reform, about 1,638,000 families acquired land.

Unfortunately, land reform did not increase agricultural output in a satisfactory way. The main reason was the smallness of pieces of land that each peasant received. Sixty-eight percent of the farmers received pieces of land less than 5 hectares, while the minimum profitable for agricultural activity was estimated at 7 hectares. Therefore, the fourth phase of land reform was designed in order to consolidate small holdings into optimum sizes.

The new policy either encouraged farmers to participate in the new-run farming corporations, or it forced them to put their land at the disposal of private agricultural firms established by Iranian and foreign investment. The purpose of this was to increase productivity by using intensive capital techniques in the countryside.

Legislation regarding farm corporations was approved by Madjliss in 1967, and until the spring of 1973, forty-three corporations had been created on the model of the United States agricultural-business corporations. The purpose of this policy was to introduce modern mechanized farming techniques and also to consolidate uneconomic holdings into units of at least 20 hectares. Under the 1967 law, if 51% of the landowners that are eligible for such corporations give their consent, then the corporation should be formed. Participating members received shares in the corporation, and use of their lands passed to the hands of the corporation, and power resided with the state appointed managers. This process created discontent among the peasants who felt that what the government gave them would be taken away in the future; and therefore, they were discouraged to invest in agriculture and increase their output. Investment in agriculture decreased because of these unfavorable effects in organizing corporations.

In Khosistan, some farm corporations were set up with Iranian and foreign capital, and the majority of foreign capital in corporations belonged to Americans. At Haft-teppes in Khosistan, a large corporation was formed for the cultivation of cane-sugar. For example, a large corporation was established by Hashemi Naraghi, an Iranian ex-patriot who owned 51% of corporate shares and 30% of the National City Bank, (the remaining shares divided among the smaller Iranian interests. 20,000 hectares of land were put at the disposal of this corporation. This policy was not met with success because mechanization created large unemployment in rural areas, and because of immense overhead expenses, it was not profitable. Naraghi and other foreign investors later on sold their shares to the government and left the country. This experience proved that beyond a certain point the scale of economics did not normally hold in agriculture, and medium size farms were more profitable.

Land reform that was put into action in order to create equality among the farmers and increase output, was a failure in Iran because in pratice, it created more inequalities and agricultural products did not increase satisfactorily.

The reason for the failure of land reform in Iran are as follows: 50% of the peasants did not benefit from land reform because the previous structure of the countryside was used as a basis for land reform, therefore only those peasants who possessed agricultural tools or animals benefited from it, and as a result, a class of farm bourgeois was formed; and the farm proletariat increased in numbers.

The farm bourgeois consisted of some previous landowners who had retained their land by different ways, rich farmers owning land, and shopkeepers and money lenders in rural areas. The proletariat's class comprised of peasants without land or having very small holdings without having agricultural tools or animals. After the land reform in the countryside of Iran, the capitalistic system with it's modern technique farming system existed together with the farming of traditional methods.

One important effect of the land reform was the increased government intervention in agricultural activity; so that the government was not only responsible for redistributing land and regulating relations between farmers and owners of land, but it also had a great role in providing credit for agriculture and administrating cooperative firms. Agricultural output did not increase after the land reform, so the government was obliged to enlarge it's intervention in order to control production and participate in farm cooperatives and farm corporations. Consequently, after the land reform, the government succeeded the landlords.

In 1963, the government also established a literary corps in the countryside and between 1963 and 1971, 62,730 young men served in the literary corps in military service, and in 1969 a woman's education corps was also established. Over this period 13,782 elementary schools were established in villages and the total number of peasants attending these shcools rose from 675,000 in 1963 to 1,830,000 in 1971.

In 1964, the health corps was established. This institution provided a national service where boys and girls not engaged in military service participated. The health corps in the first three years of it's existence, established 500 medical units in the countryside that were mobile and each of them covered many villages.

During the land reform period, about 6,700 cooperatives were formed by the government which granted loans to members of cooperatives through the Agricultural Bank of Iran with an interest rate of 7%. Mostly rich farmers were able to receive these loans and they relented them to poor farmers at higher rates. The ordinary peasant usually had to borrow money from money lenders at the excessive rate which was sometimes more than 50%.

We can say that the government by implementing it's land reform program and credit policy, strengthened only the farm bourgeois, and usually the directors of the farms were the rich farmers.

After the land reform, previous landlords were integrated in the city and became the first group of bourgeois farmers who used their capital for buying and selling land in towns and big cities. This kind of activity enabled them to acquire more profit in comparison with other kinds of economic activities, and as a result, the price of land and rents increased.

The important features of Iran's land reform were: First, it was selective and it's effectiveness was based on the previous systems; secondly, the government became the most powerful economic as well as political power in the Iranian countryside. After land reform, the peasants were powerless as before. Their boss had changed from landlord to government.

<u>Successes and failures of Iran's land reform-</u>

It has been shown in previous pages, as a result of implementing the land reform, capitalism had been imposed on the Iranian countryside and by the unequal distribution of land under increased state control.

We are trying to examine here, the results of the land reform in Iran in comparison to what other devloping countries (capitalist or socialist) achieved by land reform. In this analysis, we should consider not only the political effects, but also the reform's contribution to the economic development of Iran.

The following discussion is based on six criteria; four of them primarily economic; and the other two socio-political, briefly explaining the most important ways in which an agrarian transformation can help an overall development:

1- The increase of supply of agricultural products to meet increasing demand: An underdeveloped country requires increased output to feed it's people and provide raw materials for industries, and to export in order to finance imports of capital goods. Usually this purpose is achieved by an increase in productivity through changes in the methods of cultivation, introduction of fertilizers and new seeds, and also, the transfer of excessive peasants to other sectors.

Considering the population growth of an annual 3% and per capita increase, demand for consumption of food in Iran especially meat and diary products, rapidly increased and agricultural products were urgently needed, but Iranian performance in this field was unsatisfactory. Since 1960, agricultural products in this country had risen about 2%, and in some years even 1%, which is below the annual population growth of the country.

By the middle of 1970, the demand for agricultural products was rising by 12% and reached to 14%. Demand for meat rosed in the year 1974 more than 100%. It is not surprising that after the land reform, the shortage of agricultural products was felt intensely in Iran. In other countries, in the immediate aftermath of land reform, shortage of agricultural products were common. In China, for example, the available supply of food fell by 33% in the year following the collectivization of land, but in Iran, weakness of agriculture had continued in later years and agricultural products did not increase.

Table 2: Production indices of Iranian agriculture 1961-1973

year (1)	total agriculture (100 1961-1965)	per capita agr.(100*1961-5)
1961-5	100	100
1964	97	94
1965	105	99
1966	110	101
1967	122	109
1968	133	115
1970	128	108
1971	131	107
1972	127	100
1972	133	102
1973	135	101

Source: United States Department Of Agriculture,1974

As a result of the food shortage, the government was faced with a choice either to decreased supply and thereby create dissatisfaction among the people, or import food in order to meet the increasing demands. The government chosed the latter, and used a part of the oil income to import food. This policy was pursued also in later years. Every year the food imports increased and the country became more and more dependent on foreign countries to feed its people. The government in order to avoid further discontent, also implemented a food subsidy program which cost three billion dollars in the year of 1974. Food imports in 1977 were 2.6 billion dollars and rose in 1980 to 4 billion dollars, about one third of Iran's food requirement.

Table 3: Aricultural production and imports in 1974-1975 (in metric tons)

Commodity	Iranian production	imports
real meat	510,000	24,000
chickens	112,000	200
eggs	143,800	8,000
wheat	4,700,000	1,485,000
barley	900,000	178,000
rice	950,000	176,000
jute	3,000	10,000
silk	3,200	8,700

Source: Iran Economic Service- Echo, Tehran

The oil income provided the money to finance food imports and temporarily stopped the increase of its prices, but at the same time, it caused Iranian agriculture to remain inefficient and weak. There were several reasons for the insufficient agriculture in Iran, the most important of which are: unfavorable physical climate and soil that limited increasing output, rain shortage leaving most of Iran's desert uncultivable. There was also the fact that although owernership of land was changed, there was no change for the better in cultivation methods and by abolition of the traditional Nassagh system that previously enabled peasants to work together in teams, had not been replaced. The government failed throughout the 1960's to inject enough capital into agriculture. In 1969, for example, only six percent of the total investment went into agriculture. Under the fifth plan, agricultural credit was increased but much of the money allocated went to rich peasants,and it was used mostly for short term needs. The peasants used sixty-five percent of the credits on uses other than agriculture, mostly for remarrying or going on pilgrimages. We can say that the vast and corrupt administration did nothing to improve agriculture, and the peasants themselves for historical reasons were inactive, and did nothing to improve production.

2- Structuring the labor market: In the employment situation, there is a great difference between the requirements of earlier and later industrializing countries. In earlier instances, industries were mostly labor intensive and population growth was lower. To increase agricultural productivity and meet the labor demand of the industry, it was necessary to transfer excessive labor from agriculture to be employed in urban industries. But at the present time in underdeveloped countries, the reverse is the case. The reason is that industry today is more capital intensive and the population is growing faster than the requirements of urban employment. Today, land reform should provide employment opportunity in the countryside for the increased peasant population and the absolute number of farmers should not be decreased. Most developing countries who implemented a land reform program failed to resolve this problem which resulted in the migration of peasants to towns wihout employment opportunity, together with the countryside continuing to have considerable amount of unemployed and underemployed peasants. This phenomenom not only represented an immense waste of human resources, but also had very unfavorable political and social consequences in towns.

The percentage of the labor force employed in agriculture in Iran had fallen from 56% in 1956 to 33% in 1976. But the absolute number of labor in agriculture increased from 3,326,000 in 1956 to 3,445,000 in 1976. This shows the fact that the population had risen so rapidly in Iran that agriculture had to sustain it's absolute level of employment. According to an estimate of the Iranian Labor Organization, it was necessary to create 1.5 million new jobs in Iran provided there was no reduction in agricultural employment. Mechanization had already reduced the number of employed and in areas where agricultural activity was done by traditional methods, there existed about 40% underemployment.

3- Expanding home market and creating equality of incomes: There is no doubt that after land reform, markets for industrial products increased in the countryside, and agricultural products increased in the towns market, but rapid growth created many problems.

First of all, instead of the peasants supplying their increased products to the towns, they consumed more themselves, or they used their money on goods other than the products for the industrial sector.

Secondly, the unequal distribution of land necessarily led to inequalities in income and 50% of the population that did not receive land had not seen their income rise considerably. Before the increase of the oil income as table 4 shows, 80% of the peasants had 200 dollars per capita income and their average income did not exceed 100 dollars and 60% of the farmers had a yearly consumption of 150 dollars. After the increase of the oil income, the income of the urban dwellers increased rapidly and as a result, the difference between the income of the people living in towns and the countryside, previously about 200% increased to 800%. This showed that the peasants had not benefited neither from land reform nor from the increase of the oil income.

Cooperatives were established in villages after the land reform, but were not able to establish linkage between the agricultural sector and the industrial sector, as well as they had failed in every degree to market the produce of their farm members. They also did not succeed to provide their members with the necessary inputs, and they remained only credit giving organizations.

The agricultural purchase from the industry was 15% of it's input, while industrial purchases were about 30% of its requirements from domestic agriculture. The weak linkage between agriculture and industry was one of the reasons for the slow growth of agriculture in Iran.

Table 4: Per capita of rural income and expenditure 1972 (U.S. dollar per capita)

Category	income mean income	% of rural population	
more than 400	1,000	1.2	(farmers with over 50 hectares)
200-400	302	19.2	(animal herders and 11-50 hectares)
100-200	131	32.9	(3-10 hectares)
less than 100	70	46.7	(less than 3 hectares and landless)
		100	

Expenditure	
more than 395	2.2
296-395	2.2
211-316	6.9
123-247	30.3
89-148	33.6
less than 133	24.8
	100

Source: World Bank, The Economic Development Of Iran- Volume 2, 1974

4- Generating a surplus- The conventional way for a developing country to industrialize, is to take the surplus out of agriculture through taxation or forced acquisition, (as in Russia and China), and use it to feed the labor in industries. The oil income saved Iran by generating it's surplus from agriculture, but this does not mean that agriculture had no role in providing the surplus for industrialization.

Under Reza Shah's reign, agriculture provided 20% of the revenue and this helped him to carry out the limited industrialization of the 1930's. After the land reform, as a result of depressed agriculture, not only agricultural tax was reduced, but it has been said that, a vast amount of the oil income was used to import agricultural products and to subsidize foods in order to stabilize its prices. Considering that oil is an exhaustible resource, it is necessary that agriculture create enough funds in the long run in order to develop itself.

The above mentioned four functions of land reform are predominantly economic but the following two are mostly political and social problems.

5- Transforming the old land owning class- In Iran, some of the landowners conserved their land through different ways and became part of the rural bourgeois, Other land owners who lost their lands, were active in buying and selling land in big cities especially in Tehran, participated in commerce and industrial activities and so became a part of urban bourgeois. Therefore, we can conclude that after land reform, previous land owners did not disappear but were transformed into agricultural, industrial and commercial capitalists and some of them became government employees.

6- Stabilizing social and political conditions in rural areas- The United States government supported Iran's land reform policy in order to avoid revolution in Iran. Also, the Shah implemented land reform programs to encourage peasants to support his regime. Certainly, there was no danger of revolt from the peasants in Iran during this short period of time, but it was considered that in the long run, that land reform was necessary to establish stability in rural areas.

Past experience proves that if land reform is implemented correctly, the general consent of peasants is acquired, and as a substitute to revolution, industrial evolution on the contrary, would make conditions favorable.

Because of the shortage of land in Iran, from the distribution of land among peasants thus creating two separate classes in rural areas, i.e. rural bourgeois and rural proleteriat, there should be in each village, one cooperative that would aid in the increase of production. After the land reform, a great number of peasants who had not received land emigrated to the town and created difficulties for the town's administration because of the shortage of water, housing and electricities and other amenities.

As a result of a great increase in population and per capita income in Iran every year after land reform, imports of food and other agricultural products increased enormously, so that in the later years of the 1970's, the value of food imports was six times the value of agricultural exports. One third of domestic consumption consisted of rice, wheat and sugar, and 75% of the oil was imported from foreign countries. Ten years before, Iran was the net exporter of wheat, rice and cotton.

Cooperatives were established in villages, but because of a lack of efficient management, and the farm corporation's incorrect planning; all were doomed to failure and as a result, the country became greatly dependent on food and agricultural raw materials from foreign countries.

CHAPTER 6

IRAN'S INDUSTRIAL DEVELOPMENT AND OIL INDUSTRY

Since the early 1960's, when the government began to promote economic development in a concerted manner, Iran's economy underwent a major transformation and achieved great successes. All the conventional indications of growth demonstrated this: In terms of current prices the Gross National Product rosed by 8% per year in the 1960's, by 14.2% in 1972-3, by 30.3% in 1973-4, and by 42% in 1974-5. Between 1972 and 1978, the G.N.P. grew from 17.3 billion dollars to 54.6 billion dollars. Per capita income also increased from 450 dollars in 1971 to 2400 dollars in 1978.

During the above period, the industrial sector developed immensely and had an average of 14 to 17% annual growth rate. It occupied an important place in the economy of the country, employing nearly a quarter of the labor force and accounting for 16% of the G.N.P.

Although the official statistics of economic and industrial growth was exaggerated and also having in mind that some part of the growth was related to the increase of oil income, and price increases, neverthless; there is no doubt that Iran's growth rate was exceptional and was one of the highest among the third world capitalist or socialist countries.

Certainly, the rapid growth rate of the economy was due: first of all, to the increase of the oil income, and therefore the growth of the economy of the country gained a greater dependence every year on the oil income. In 1967, the oil income represented 17% of the G.N.P., and in 1977 it rosed to 38%. -In 1977, about 77% of the government revenue and 87% of the exchange revenue of the country was provided by the oil income. The oil income rosed from 2 billion dollars in 1972 to 20 billion in 1976.

Although oil provided opportunity for rapid growth, on the other hand, it imposed some important limits on economic development as follows:

1- The oil industry in Iran had no significant linkage with the rest of the economy, because being capital intensive; it employed a tiny labor force, and acquired it's capital and technology from abroad. Even in early years of it's development, food requirements of employees and labor were imported from abroad. Furthermore a major part of the oil products were exported while only providing the source of energy for domestic use, and therby saved the foreign exchange that would otherwise be used in importing the needed oil. Oil had an important effect on the economy by providing income for the government in hard currencies. Therefore, the real effect of the oil income on the economy depended on how the government spent the oil income.

2- Injecting oil money into the economy of the country usually intensified inflation. Incomes of different groups of people became more unequal, unproductive activities such as speculation of land increased, unhealthy and uncompetitve industries came into existence, and as a result of those unfavorable developments, government had no choice but to use the oil income to import consumer goods instead of investing it in productive projects. Since oil is an exhaustible resource, it must be considered as capital and not as income, and it must be replaced by another kind of capital.

Industrial Development

During the reign of Reza Shah, the government of Iran by establishing control on foreign trade and exchange control, and creating other facilities; made the environment of Iran favorable for the development of industries; and as a result of this policy, nearly 200 industrial plants were established in the country between 1934 and 1940, that employed between 50,000 to 60,000 workers. In the private sector, the largest number of industries produced textiles while the state owned military factories manufactured sugar, cement, tobacco and textiles. The main part of the industrial growth took place since the mid 1960's. In ten years (1965-1975), industry grew at an average rate of 15% per year in Iran. In 1977, their existed about 250,000 manufacturing establishments employing 2.5 million workers.

Apart from the petrochemical and oil industry, (that we will discuss in more detail), there were other major units as the steel mill in Isphahan and the automobile, truck, bus industry, machine tool factories and electronic assembly plants in Ahvaz. Automobilie output rose from 2300 in 1964 to 73,000 cars, 1911 buses and 29.365 trucks in 1974-5(a part of it was exported). The aim of the automobile industry was to produce two million automobiles of all kinds by the end of the sixth plan in 1983.

1- The government had invested large amounts of money for creating necessary infrastructure for industrial development such as, constructing roads, ports, dams, and providing electricity and water. The government also had made direct industrial investments and participated with the private sector to establish heavy industries such as iron-mills, machine tool factories, and petrochemical plants. Under the third plan, 53.1% of all industrial investments were made by the state, 38.8% under the fourth plan and under the fifth plan 40%.

In 1973, as a result of the oil price increase, government investment rose to 60%. The main part of the government investment was earmarked to petro-chemical, steel and transportation industries. Secondly, by creating specialized banks such as two industrial banks and also through Bank Mellie Gran, government provided necessary funds for private sector for investment in projects that has been assigned to that sector.

Table 5: Industrial output

	units	1969	1971	1973	1975(1st 9mos)
glass plates	1,000 tons	17.7	30.6	86.9	59.5
passenger cars	1,000 units	28.3	38.9	49.8	68.0
trucks-station wagons	units	5089.0	12313.0	23258.0	33580.0
busses & minibuses	units	3161.0	3008.0	5007.0	3482.0
trailers	units	961.0	586.0	1133.0	978.0
tractors	units	399.0	3833.0	7124.0	6500.0
refrigerators	1,000 units	176.8	192.5	324.0	332.8
electrical appl.	1,000 units	5832.0	6374.0	25237.0	25336.0
television sets	1,000 units	87.3	150.0	218.8	230.4
coolers	1,000 units	64.1	122.7	139.4	126.3
water heaters	1,000 units	42.9	55.6	83.7	98.0
cement	million tons	2.3	2.8	3.3	3.8
paint	1,000 tons	14.1	16.9	22.4	24.0
carboard	1,000 tons	10.0	13.1	12.9	10.5
beer	million litres	25.8	29.7	39.0	41.2

Source: Bank Markazi Of Iran

Thirdly, the government through granting tax exemptions and imposing import duties on goods similar to domestic products as high as 200% (an average of 80%) and exempting the imports of machine tools and raw materials necessary for industries, had encouraged the growth of domestic industries. In an attempt to reduce pressure on the Tehran region, the government gave extra encouragements and exemptions to industries established outside 120 kilometers of Tehran.

The second factor that induced the industrialization of Iran, was the private sector. In the past, the private capitalist activity in Iran was mostly commerce, and only after land reform, with government encouragement, some private persons concentrated their activity in light industries and house building; and it's existence was dependent mostly on state funds and state encouragements. Since the 1950's, a small industrial bourgeois group gradually formed in Iran. In 1974, forty-five families owned 85% of private industrial firms. This group was comprised of ex-landowners, former bazaar traders and some high officials of government who had acquired wealth through savings or corruption. The private sector in Iran mostly invested in safe projects and in industries that the government protected and supported.

The third factor in promoting industrialization in Iran was foreign capital. In the past, the only significant foreign investment in Iran was in oil. In 1955, the Central Bank established a center for attracting and promotion foreign investments, and a law was passed by Madjliss regarding the encouragement of foreign investments.

According to the above law, a number of guarantees were accorded to the foreign firms. They were granted a five year exemption from taxation, the right to repatriate profits in the currency in which they first made investmets, and the exemption from duty on necessary imports for running the industrial plants. Consequently, by the mid-1970's, over 200 foreign firms had invested in Iran. In 1975, the United States invested in Iran a total of 589 million rials, Germany-238 million rials, England-135 million rials, France-629 million rials, Japan-1707 million rials, and the others 678 million rials all totalling 3976 million rials.

Foreign investment in Iran was 23% in petrochemical, 17% in automobile, 16.5% tire manufacturing, 13% in metal factories, 6.6% in agriculture and 4.2% in house and apartment buildings. The greatest foreign investment was made by Japan (43%) and the main part of it was in petrochemicals. The main aim of attracting foreign investment was to have access to advance technology, management and marketing facilities, but because of the oil income, foreign funds were not urgently needed for financing development projects. Under the fifth plan, it was decided that the state invest 46.2 billion dollars and foreign investment was only 2.8 billion dollars during this plan.

While the foreign firms were guaranteed favorable terms, at the same time, in order to protect the national interest, the government imposed some very strict terms, for example, foreign firms were authorized to operate only through joint ventures with Iranian partners, and could only have minority shares in those ventures. After the workers share program was introduced in 1975, foreign investors had an average of 25% holdings. Despite the monopoly of technology, foreign firms had a far greater power than their shares permitted.

Although profits of Iranian and foreign firms were very high, as much as 50% per annum, the relationship between the state and the industrial firms was uneasy. This was one of the factors that restricted industrial growth in Iran. First of all, investors had to spend too much time getting industrial permits, and they were obliged to bribe officials that were in charge of granting those permits. They had to cope with the government and contradictory regulations. On the whole, the Iranian administration had not properly converted to the needs of the rapid economic development; and so the flow of information and cooperation between private sector and the state was not in satisfactory condition. In 1977, when the state was not capable of extending loans and credits, because of the falling oil income, foreign firms sold their shares and pulled out of Iran altogether.

The government of Iran, in order to support and encourage industrial investments, was faced with a dilemma: To induce investments, it was necessary to insure high profits for the investors, on the other hand, to protect consumers, it had to limit profits and prevent an increase of prices. A clear instance of this conflict of policies appeared in 1975, when the government, in order to protect the interest of consumers and workers, launched three distinct campaigns, one against price profiteering, one against corruption, and one to establish the worker's share in industries.

The share program was also intended to encourage laborers to stay where they were working. The price campaign led to the arrest and fining of over 8000 Iranian businessmen. There were also charges of corruption against some foreign firms such as, the German, American and Simens (a German firm). The workers share program was seen by private investors as a threat to their position. As a result of the above policies, domestic and foreign investment decreased and in 1975, during a few weeks, more than two billion dollars left the country.

Table 6: Foreign private investment in Iran by country of origin (million rials)

country of origin	1968-9	1970-1	1973-4	1974-5	1975-6
U.S.A.	855	560	1090	797	589
West Germany	178	720	662	130	238
U.K.	242	331	25	52	135
France	67	117	23	61	629
Japan	-	129	1659	2867	1707
others	141	461	585	593	678
Total	1483	2318	4044	4500	3976

Table 7: Private foreign investment in Iran by type of activity and countries, 1975-6 (percent)

Activity	Percent
Agroindustry	6.6
mining	0.3
food	0.3
rubber	16.4
pharmaceuticals and chemical	6.4
petrochemicals	22.9
metallurgical	6.9
electrical and electronic industries	6.3
automobile industry and transporation	17.0
building materials and construction	4.2
hotels and others	12.7
Total	100.0
From	
United States	14.8
United Kingdom	3.4
Germany	6.0
France	15.8
Japan	42.9
Others	17.1
Total	100.0

Source: Annual report and balance sheet of Bank Bank Markazi, Iran

In 1977, the growth rate decreased, as a result of falling oil exports, depression of agriculture and lack of sufficient electric power. According to statistics published by Bank Markazi of Iran, it was only 2.8%, while in 1976 it was 34% and in 1975, about 40%. This proves that the main part of rapid growth in the previous years was also due to the increase of the oil income and to some extent to the price increases. But if we consider the oil income as capital and not as income, then the real growth rate would be much less than what was claimed during recent years by the Iranian government.

Iran's oil industry

Discovery and production of oil in Iran began in 1908, earlier than any other Persian Gulf countries. After the second world war, it's output had risen considerably and reached in 1975 to 5.4 million barrels per day, ranking among middle east producers as the second to Saudi Arabia. The main producing area is the southern province of Khosistan and in 1975, thirty major wells were in operation in that province, 19 on land and 11 offshore.

Iranian oil reserves was estimated to be sixty billion barrels and at the rate of the 1975 production, it would last about thirty years. The oil reserves of Iraq, Saudi Arabia and Kuviet are substantially higher than Irans reserves, hence, they would be capable of exporting oil much longer than Iran. Considering the increasing consumption of oil in Iran, because of it's large and growing population; it is estimated that Iran's oil export would decrease in the early years of the 1990's.

Exploitation of the oil occurred in Iran until 1951, by an Anglo-Persian ôil company that was paying Iran an insignificant part of its profits. Even after renewing the agreement in 1933, during Reza Shah's reign, revenues of Iran from this source was very small. The monopoly agreement of oil production between Iran and the Anglo-Persian oil company was in two ways a disadvantage to Iran. First of all, Iran received a very low income and secondly, the volume of oil production and export was not determined by Irans own policies and needs, but by the the needs of the company. As long as Iran's oil industry was in the hands of the above foreign company, it was administered as a foreign industry, and it had no interest in the industrial development of the country. After the second world war, a growing movement in Iran led by a prominent spokesman, Mohammad Mossadegh, organized the nationalization movement. In 1951, the oil industry was nationalized by parliment and Dr. Mossadegh was appointed as prime minister to implement the nationalization act. While the Iranian government and the British Petroleum Company failed to agree on the terms of the settlement, the British Petroleum Company with the cooperation of the oil cartel succeeded in boycotting the sale of Iranian oil in the world markets and consequently the export of oil ceased.

In 1954, after Mossadegh's government was overthrown, an agreement was reached with the International Consortium that was formed for this purpose. The oil industry after the above agreement was still nationalized, but the effective control over the two important issues, price and output, lay in the hands of the foreigners. In the Consortium, British Petroleum retained 40% of the shares and the Shell Company acquired 14%, five main American oil companies shared 40% and C.F.P. 6%. This was the way the oil operation of Iran was Internationalized. Some non-basic operations(service operations) and distribution of oil inside the country was transferred to the Iranian Oil company. According to the agreement, the Consortiums operations were limited to it's area of current production, so the Iranian Oil company (N.I.C.C.) invited other independent companies and concluded with them contracts on terms more favorable to Iran to exploit oil in other areas. But these companies did not succeed in discovering sufficient quantities of oil, and their production accounted for only 4% of Iran's oil output in 1975.

More fundamental changes took place in the Iranian Oil industry in the early 1970's. The Organization of Petroleum Exporting Countries (OPEC) was established in 1960 and Iran was one of the countries that joined it at the time of it's inception. Throughout the decade of the 1960's, the price of oil had remained static, but at the beginning of the 1970's, the OPEC countries by limiting production were able to raise the price of oil many times. On several occasions, the price of oil was raised from 1.79 dollars per barrel in 1971, to 11.65 in December 1973. The Shah of Iran presiding over an OPEC meeting in February 1971 in Tehran, asked for a price raise and by coordinated efforts of all members of OPEC; the price of oil increased considerably. At that time, two countries had the most significant influence in OPEC, Iran supporting a higher rise in the oil price and Saudi Arabia defending a moderate advance, for example, in 1976, Iran was asking for a 10% rise of the oil income, but Saudi Arabia was content with a 5% increase.

As a result of the oil price increase, Iranian revenues from the oil export increased substantially from less than 2 billion dollars in 1971 to more than 20 Billion in 1976. In addition, the Iranian government acquired effective control over the output of the oil industry through a renegotiation of the 1954 agreement, and other countries of OPEC members did nearly the same thing. The new agreement gave N.I.O.C. full control of output throughout the area, previously controlled by the Consortium, and officially the role of foreign oil companies was limited to providing some technical services and purchasing of Iranian oil.

The Iranian government claims that due to the new agreement Iran acquired it's full independence in production and marketing of it's oil, but critics have the opinion that the oil companies still control Iranian oil. Neither of these views are accurate, because the degree of power exerted by Iran over the industry increased considerably while at the same time the foreign companies retained some power, with their marketing facilities and technological expertise.

Table 8: Iranian oil revenues

Output per barrel		(m$) income	Output per barrel		(m$) income
1938	203,900	17	1972	5,067,000	2,308
1950	635,000	45	1973	5,896,000	5,600
1960	1,020,000	285	1974	6,021,000	18,523
1969	3,044,000	908	1975	5,350,000	18,871
1970	3,845,000	1,093	1976	5,899,000	20,488
1971	4,566,000	1,870	1978	4,900,000	17,000

Source: Financial Times

The N.I.O.C. besides developing its operations in Iran gradually extended it's activity to foreign countries and became one of the important oil companies in the world. For instance, it installed refineries and fertilizer factories in some other countries such as India, South Korea and South Africa. Prior to the increase of the oil price, the N.I.O.C. was inclined to build many refineries in Iran and in other countries, because at that time, the profit of selling refined oil was more than the profit of selling raw oil. After the increase of the oil price, due to the existence of the excess capacity of refinery in the world; and imposing high duties for the import of refined oil in most countries, the process of refining oil would not be a sufficient profit, therefore, the Iranian National Oil company decreased its efforts in achieving this purpose.

Table 9: Iran's investment in the oil industry (Million dollars)

	1358	1357	1358	1359
exploration & production	980	1886	1051	-
oil refinery	377	218	235	-
transportation & distribution	284	198	143	500
Total	1,641	2,302	1,429	500

Source: N.I.O.C. Report

Under the fifth plan, 11.7 billion dollars was allocated for the investment in the oil industry and a substantial part of it (9.7) billion dollars was assigned to the exploration activity especially designed for re-exploitation of the oil wells, and also taking into consideration the increase of domestic consumption of refined oil, a considerable amount of funds were allocated for building refineries in Iran.

After the revolution, the amount of investment in oil decreased substantially and activities for re-exploitation of the wells and repairing and maintenance of the oil installation stopped. Undoubtedly, the sharp decrease of investment in oil especially in the field of re-exploiting wells and maintenance of installations would in the future, present great difficulties and a substantial part of oil that is exploitable would be lost forever.

Petrochemical Industries

In the 1960's, as a result of a continual decrease of the oil price in world markets, Iranian authorities became interested in creating a petrochemical industry. They argued that Irans vast resources of oil and gas could be used as raw material in petrochemical industries and thereby retaining for herself the extra value of selling the products of the industries.

The first such plant called "Petrochemical Complex" was built in 1961 in the city of Shiraz. The petrochemical company of Iran was established for the purpose of developing petrochemical industries. This company encouraged domestic and foreign investment in this field and was supporting them in many ways. Consequently, five petrochemical plants with the participation of foreign and domestic investment were established in the country.

In 1977, Iran was capable of producing three million tons of various petrochemical products and earned 250 million dollars from exporting some of it. The government expected the petrochemical industry to become in the future, the most important source of exchange earning after the oil industry. At the beginning of the revolution, total value of the petrochemical plants in Iran exceeded 3 billion dollars.

The most important petrochemical plants in Iran are as follows:

1- The Fertilizer Company Of Iran- This plant that belonged to the Petrochemical Company of Iran, is situated in Marvdasht near Shiraz and its yearly productions are: 52,000 tons of eureh, 30,000 nitrate amoniac, 4,000 tons of nitrate acid, 53,000 tons of soda ash, 1,000 tons of bicarbonate sodium, 50,000 tons of mixed fertilizer, 30,000 tons of phosphate sodium and 41,500 tons of amoniac. It was decided that during the fifth plan to spend 460 million dollars to increase the capacity of this plant considerably.

2- Petrochemical Company Of Abadan- This firm was created by participation of the Iran Petrochemical Company by 74%, B.F. Goodrich, an American company by 26% and it produced plastic material, chemical powder and dishwashing powder for domestic uses.

3- Petrochemical Company of Shapour- This company was created by investment of the Iran Petrochemical Company, and produces: fertilizer, sulfur and sulfuric acid. It utilizes as raw material, gas and phosphate that is imported from abroad. Until the revolution about 350 million dollars had been spent for building its installations, and after completion, it would be able to produce: 600 tons of amoniac, 595 tons of sulfur, 710 tons of ureh, 1000 tons of sulfuric acid and 260 tons of phosphoric acid.

4- Petrochemical Company Of Khark- This firms was created by 50% participation of the Iran Petrochemical Company, and 50% from Amoco Company, an american firm. In 1977, it produced 185 tons of sulfur, 1.3 million barrels of protein, 800,000 barrels of butane and 1.2 million barrels of natural gasoline and exported a main part of it's produce to other countries.

5- Iran Carbon Company- 20% of the shares of this company belonged to Iran Petrochemical Company, 50%

the Cabut Corporation, 10% to the Industrial and Mining Bank of Iran and 10% to the International Finance Corporation and the remaining 10% to the private sector. This plant is situated in Ahwaz and produces 16 tons of black carbon yearly.

Unifinished projects

1- The Petrochemical Complex of Iran and Japan- Iran holds 50% shares of this project. Mitsubish 24%, and Nisho 26%, both Japanese companies. This project is the largest petrochemical complex in the middle east and it's site is Bandarshahpour. At first, the expenses of building this project was estimated at 1.8 billion dollars, but later on, it increased considerably. Before the revolution, 85% of this project was completed. This complex comprised of salt electrolysing factories, is capable of producing 60 tons of soda per year, 200,000 tons of chlorine gas, and a considerable quantity of olifin. After completion, this project should create 3000 jobs and produce 2.8 million tons of petrochemical products to the value of nearly one billion dollars. Installation of this project was greatly damaged by the war between Iran and Iraq, and because of the prevailing insecurity in the area, the Japanese specialists left the country after the revolution and completion of this project stopped.

2- Aromatic Factory in Abadan- This factory was created in Abadan for producing perfumes and it's capacity after completion should be 760 tons of various perfumes per year.

In addition to the above projects, some projects such as the Fibre Company, and the Pazargad Chemical Company are projected by the private sector to be carried out in the future.

From experience, petrochemical companies in Iran because of the weakness of the economy and enormous expenses of installations, and existence of extra capacity of production in the world, had not made the success anticipated, despite the investment of more than 3 billion dollars, it's income is not significant. Also, most of the third world countries that built petrochemical industries were faced with the same problems that plaqued Iran. The reasons are: this industry requires enormous investments, and the optimum (minimum economical) capacity is large, in addition, it needs complex technology, efficient management and skilled marketing. Developing countries can only provide these requirements by having foreign partners. Furthermore, in Iran, as in other developing countries, costs are twice as much as in a developed country. Japan, for instance can neutralize the advantage of having cheap raw materials. On the other hand, because of the smallness of the domestic market, the main part of the produce must be exported and because of the excess capacity in the world markets and the existence of high tariffs, exports were faced with difficulties.

Because of the enormous investments made in the past, Iran should complete the unfinished products and use a great part of these goods in domestic markets.

CHAPTER 7

ENERGY POLICY

ENERGY POLICY

At the present, the advanced countries, knowing that the oil reserves would be exhausted probably in the early decades of the next century, are diversifying their energy policy by taking into consideration, their other resources as coal, gas, atomic power, etc. The Iranian government is anticipating that its oil reserves at the rate of current production would last only three decades, decided before the revolution to base it's policy of energy in the future, on it's vast gas and other reserves. This policy is discussed here in the following pages:

The gas industry

In addition to oil, Iran had vast reserves of

gas. In 1980, the proven gas reserves were estimated around 490 trillion cubic feet, that is nearly 20% of the worlds gas reserves and ranked as second after Russia among the worlds countries. Luckily, the most part of these reserves were exploitable and about half of it was mixed with oil. Nearly half of the country's gas reserves are in Khosistan, and in one of its areas called Pars Gas, it is estimated to have more than 54 trillion cubic feet of gas reserves.

The energy value of Iran's gas reserves is estimated to be the equivalent to the value of 82 billion barrels of oil, namely 41% more than the value of Iran's proven oil reserves. Therefore, Iran has more prestige in this field than any other middle east country. Iran's operation of exploration and extraction of gas is run by the Iran oil company and marketing is operated only by Iran's gas corporation.

Exploitation of gas not mixed with oil began in the 1970's, but still, activities in this field are not high. In 1975 and 1976, 28 wells had been exploited and gas produced from these wells was used for domestic consumption, as raw material for petrochemical industries and for injection into oil wells. The majority of the exploited gas had been mixed with oil.

In the past, the gas mixed with oil was burned and wasted, but from 1973 to 1978, the wasted gas decreased from 60% to 46%. Nevertheless, in 1978, about 1.96 trillion cubic feet of gas burned in flames, During the same period, injection of gas into oil wells increased from 2% in 1976 to 18% in 1978.

Before the revolution, the government had a program to prevent the gradual burning of gas and to stop it completely in 1980. But after the revolution, production of gas was reduced and today the main part of it is burning in flames and is wasted. Furthermore, activities for exploration and exploitation of gas from the Pars area and the Bandarabbas and Meshad areas had completely stopped.

Table 10: Production and consumption of gas in Iran
(Trillion cubic feet)

	1973	1974	1975	1976	1977	1978
volume	1,711	1,755	1,612	1,789	2,013	1,959
percentage	100	100	100	100	100	100
exports & was.	699	792	774	763	746	692
volume %	41	45	48	43	37	36
burning volume	1,012	983	838	990	933	912
%	59	55	52	55	46	46
reinjection to oil wells						
volume				36	334	355
percentage				2	17	18

Table 11: Consumption and export of gas in 1977 (million cubic feet)

Reinjection to oil wells	330,004	volume	30.7%
export to Russia	326,903	volume	30.3%
domestic consumption	359,285	volume	33.2%

Table 12: Various items of domestic consumption of gas

Categories of consumption	Volume (m.cubic ft.)	% of total consumption
1-Fuel for production	76,166	6.9
2-Residential, commer. con. & fuel for electric plants	103,789	9.7
3-Abadan refinery	40,350	3.7
4-Shapour chemical co.	45,833	4.2
5-Used for prod. of liquid gas	75,341	7.0
6-Khark petrochemical, factory	19,779	1.8
7-Waste during Transport	61,955	5.7
Total	107,912	

At the present time, export of gas is not profitable, therefore, it should be produced primarily for domestic purposes. The first priority in using gas in the country is injecting it into oil wells in order to increase oil production and it is estimated by this process that the increase of oil will be about 25 billion barrels.

According to the agreement concluded in the 1970's between Iran and Russia, gas was exported from Iran to Russia through the pipe line called First Igaat. Also, after discovery of great gas reserves in the Pars and Kangan areas, it was decided to export gas to European countries by way of Russia, therefore, a contract was concluded for constructing a second pipe line called "Igaat 2" from Kangan to Astara. It was intended that upon completion of this pipe line the export of gas to Europe by way of Russia was to begin in 1981. It was considered also, that all of the towns situated around the second pipe line have access to nearly 1 billion square feet of gas for their energy requirements. Previous expenses of constructing the "Igaat 2" were estimated at about 2 billion dollars and many contracts were concluded between Iranian, English, French, Italian, Russian and Polish companies for constructing the pipe lines.

At the end of 1978, political disorders in Iran caused the construction of pipe lines to be postponed.

Until 1978, 700 million dollars had been spent for constructing pipe lines and later it was known that implementation of the project would cost at least 4 billion dollars.

The gas exported to Russia, first, by the pipe line is from gas mixed with oil, but it was decided to export gas to Europe by the second pipe line from gas not mixed with oil. In contracts with European countries, the price of gas was fixed at one dollar for every 1000 cubic feet. This price although higher than the gas exported to Russia was not profitable.

After the revolution, construction of the second pipe line stopped completely, because the enormous expenses of constructing the pipe line was not profitalbe. However, domestic consumption of gas and it's injection into oil wells was lucrative. Consumption of gas as energy in Iran not only provides a better and cleaner fuel, but it also frees more oil for export and provides raw material for petrochemical industries.

Gas in Iran is used for the following main purposes: petrochemical fuel for power production, fuel for industries, and heating and cooking in houses. Also, liquid gas in Iran is used in houses and in transport, prepared in capsules of 12 kilos. As the villages in Iran are very dispersed, it is advantageous to use liquid gas in capsules instead of constructing pipe lines with great expenditure. Iran's proven gas reserve is estimated to be sufficient to meet Iran's energy requirements for the next two and a half centuries.

Atomic power

After an increase of more than four times the oil price in 1973, the Shah of Iran decided to create a substantial atomic power. He argued that oil was too precious to be used as fuel and it was more probable and more profitable for it to be used in the future only as raw material for petrochemical and for export in order to earn foreign exchange. He was of the opinion that the cost of atomic power was stable, but the price of oil was increasing continuously; therefore, atomic power would be economical in the future. In addition to producing atomic power, the energy resources of the country would come from various sources and if the oil reserves were exhausted, then the country could rely mostly on atomic energy.

Certainly, there were other considerations i.e. foreign countries wanted Iran to spend their oil money immediately in order for her to become dependent on western technology. Although the Shah intended to build atomic bombs, he was anticipating these prestigious projects and their enormous expenses. The relatives of the Shah and his court also encouraged the Shah to make contracts for building atomic power in order to receive commission from the sellers of reactors.

A Canadian consultant firm called "Montreal Engineering Company," was invited by the government of Iran to study the electric power needs of Iran for the coming years. This firm had reported that the investment needed for building an atomic factory per one kilowat electric power is about 700 dollars, and Iran in 1993, would need 55,000 megawat electric power and 40% of which can be obtained from atomic power. Later, it became clear that in Iran, the necessary investment for each kilowat electricity from atomic power is much higher, 3000 to 4000 dollars, while cost of obtaining electricity from gas is only 300 dollars that is less than one tenth of atomic power.

In 1974, the Atomic Authority was established and the Shah decided to purchase 20 reactors in 20 years for Iran. At this time, investment for building

20 reactors was estimated at 100 billion dollars. The decision taken by the Shah regarding such gigantic and extravagant projects, not only needed enormous investments for many years, but it had very unfavorable environmental effects such as radiation and storage of waste. The issue was not consulted with the people and he alone decided to implement this program.

The installation of 20 reactors in Iran from an economical, social and political point of view, was not in the interest of the country, because installing atomic reactors in a dry country with frequent earthquakes, and the lack of skilled power and raw material presented great risks, but would also make Iran dependent on foreign countries for providing raw materials and technology.

It was planned, that out of 20 reactors, two were to be constructed by the German firm named, "Kraftswork Union", in the town of Bushehr, two by French companies near Karoon river, eight by the American Westinghouse company and the remaining others by German, French and British companies. Construction of two atomic reactors began by Germans in Bushehr, and a town was built for the residence of nearly

6000 German specialist and workers.

As a result of the widespread protests to extravagant investment in atomic energy and opposition of many groups in Iran, Dr. Amouzghar, prime minister at the time, appointed a committee to investigate the advantages and disadvantages of atomic energy projects. The findings of this committee are as follows:

1- Expenses of each kilowat of atomic electric power in Iran is about 3 to 4 thousand dollars. It is about 800 to 1000 dollars in industrial countries.

2- Iran does not need 20 reactors.

3- Iran can provide electric power with only 300 to 400 dollars from gas and the reserves of gas can meet Iran's requirement for more than two centuries.

4- The atomic power plants that Iran was going to purchase were too big and the electric network of the country was not capable to handle it.

5- The contracts concluded are at the country's disavantage, because all skilled workers are in the hands of foreigners and there is no possibility for Iranians to acquire nuclear technology.

6- The amount of uranium is limited in the world and Iran would be dependent in the future on foreign supplies.

7- Iran's participation in the plants of enriching uranium to the extent of 10% in French companies situated in France was also criticized by the committee, especially since the payment of 1 billion dollars had been paid by Iran even before the project began.

After the above mentioned reports, the government of Iran decided that only two atomic plants which had begun construction in Bushehr would be completed and the others were to be cancelled.

Before the revolution, 70% of the Bushehr atomic plants had been constructed and more than 6 billion marks had been spent for this purpose.

Some believed that Iran, in order to be acquainted with atomic technology and also not to be backward in comparison with neighboring countries as Pakistan, must have some reactors for scientific research. But after the revolution, only 85% of the Bushehr reactor had been completed before construction stopped.

Hydroelectric power

The prospect of the country's hydroelectric power is also helpful. In 1978, electric power produced by Iran's dams was over 1804 megawatts of which 1000 megawatts were produced by large factories of the Karoon dam, 520 megawatts by smaller factories of the Dez dam and the remaining by the Jadjrood and Arras dams. In the same year, many other dams were under construction to begin operation in 1981. At the present, 23% of the country's electric power is provided by hydroelectricity.

The hydroelectric power areas of Iran are situated mostly in mountainous areas west and north of Iran. According to a survey that was made recently, the main part of the country's electric requirements could be provided in the future by building dams on waters that originate from the Zagros mountains in Khosistan and fall in the Karoon river and also on waters that originate from the Alborz mountains and fall into the Caspian sea.

Traditional electric power

In recent years, the shortage of electric power was one of the principal factors that caused the decrease of industrial growth rate in Iran. It is necessary to sustain the growth rate to make sufficient investment for providing electric power from gas and hydroelectric sources.

At the present, the main source of electric power is from traditional sources. In 1977, about 56% of the electricity of the country was produced by gas turbines and disels. The electricity of Iran is provided both by public and private sector. Until 1960, the private sector participated in providing electricity for streets of towns, houses and commercial uses, but later on, only the government took responsibility for producing electric power for those uses, and the uses of private electricity was limited to industrial, agricultural and commercial firms. In Iran, large industrial and service units as factories, clubs, hotels and hospitals, because of having no confidence in public electric power, provided for themselves some private electric plants for emergency uses. In 1977, the share of the private sector in providing electric power of the country was only 21% of the country's total electric consumption.

Before the revolution, the capacity of electric power of the country was 7700 megawatts and it was forseen that it would increase to 20,000 megawatts in

1982. This estimation was based on producing 2400 megawatts of atomic electricity, 62% increase of hydroelectric power and tripling of traditional electric power. After the revolution, because of inadequate maintenance and repair parts, the electric plants were faced with difficulties and most of the factories were out of work and therefore, electric production had fallen to only 2500 megawatts.

During the 1970's, electric consumption had rapidly increased and it's annual growth rate was nearly 16%. Public consumption of electricity increased from 570 million kilowatts in 1972 to 14,218 million kilowatts in 1977 and the industrial sector was the main consumer (47% electricity generated by the public was consumed by industries).

Consumption of electricity in houses, in agriculture and commerce had increased in those years considerably.

In the year 1977, the private sector had produced 3300 million kilowatts and had consumed it for its own uses.

Table 12: Electric consumption in Iran
(million kilowatt in a year)

	1972	1977	% of increase
public factories including:	5723	14218	20
residential	1218	3200	21.6
commercial	1250	3200	21.2
industrial	2745	6700	20.2
agricultural	141	465	27
street lights	323	508	9.4
miscellaneous	46	145	25.6
private sector	2500	3300	9
Total	8223	17518	20

Source: Plan Oranization Annual report

CHAPTER 8

FOREIGN TRADE OF IRAN

During the decade of the 1960's, the foreign trade policy of Iran regarding imports was to encourage the imports of capital goods and raw materials required by industries and to provide the consumption of goods from domestic production and to encourage the exports of industrial products in order to make exports consist of various items.

For achieving the above goals, the following decisions were taken by the government of Iran:

1- Liberalizing, facilitating and reducing import duties of capital goods, raw materials and semi-finished goods that was required for industrialization.

2- Protecting domestic production through prohibiting the import of goods similar to the domestic products or increasing the custom duties on those goods.

3- Increasing the volume of trade with countries that had clearing and barter agreements with Iran (socialist countries) in order to encourage the exports of Iran.

4- Encouraging the increase of industrial products in order to make Irans exports more varied.

5- To conclude commercial agreements with other countries as with the common market countries and obtain from them privileges and facilities for Iran's exports.

As a result of putting into action the above policy, Iran's foreign trade during the years of 1962 until 1973 experienced an average growth rate of 16% per year. There was also fundamental changes in the composition of imports i.e., the share of consumer goods decreased and on the contrary, the share of capital goods, raw material and semi-produced goods increased. There was some important change also in the exports and for the first time, a substantial part of the exports were comprised of industrial goods.

Table 13: Iran's foreign trade during 1962-1972

year	total w.1000 tons	trade v.m. rials	imports w.1000 tons	v.m. rials	exports w.1000 tons	v.m. rials	balance
1962	2009	50508	1420	41905	5089	8603	-333-2
1966	3240	85459	2426	73644	814	11815	-61829
1972	8226	227513	5877	193651	2749	33862	-159789

Table 14: Composition of imports in the years 1968 and 1978 - value million dollars

	1968 value	%	1978 value	%	average gr.rate
intermed. goods	856.5	61.6	1526.2	62.1	17.6
capital goods	376.3	27.1	642.6	25	14.3
cons. goods	156.4	11.3	331.6	12.9	17.2
Total	1389.2	100	2570.4	100	16.7

Source: Inflation in Iran, Dr. Z. Heyat

After 1973, because of rapid increase of demand in the country and shortage of domestic products, the government was forced to change the foreign trade policy in order to facilitate the imports of consumer goods. Consequently, the imports of consumer goods increased and the exports of products decreased, as a result of demand for them at home. Unprecedented increase of imports in the years of 1973-1977 created great problems for: unloading imports, warehousing them, transporting and distribution. Port facilities were not sufficient so ships had to wait many months to unload their cargos.

Table 15: Imports and exports of the country in the years 1973 - 1975
volume: 1000 tons value: million rials

	Imports		Exports		balance
year	volume	value	volume	value	
1973	6720	253190	1885	42841	-210349
1974	9275	473219	2383	42725	-440494
1975 (nine months)	9000	682500	798	31125	-651375

Source: Inflation in Iran, Dr. Z. Heyat

Effects of the foreign trade policy on the economic development of Iran- The examination of the foreign trade policy and exchange control of Iran shows that in the last two decades, the import duties of foreign goods similar to domestic products increased continuously. In addition, other limitations such as: the requirement of deposits for ordering imports, had been imposed on the import of those goods. On the contrary, the importing of capital goods, raw material and semi-finished goods needed by domestic industries had been granted many kinds of facilities, as exemption of import duties. As a result of this policy, substantial change occurred during the implementation of the third and forth plan (1962-1973) i.e., the proportion of imported consumer goods decreased and the proportion of capital goods, raw material and semi-finished goods (excluding the years 1973-1977) increased on a regular basis. Also during this period, some fundamental industries such as, the iron mill, petrochemical and machine making factories were created by the government.

Most consumer industries such as: textile, cement, sugar, automobile, refrigerator, radio, and television industries were developed by the private sector. Most of the industries created by private capitalists were just assembly plants, and this is shown by the great increase of semi-finished goods imported in that period. In 1973, about sixty percent of the imports ($3billion) consisted of raw materials needed for domestic assembly industries and those industries had earned only 100 million dollars exchange (1/30 of it's import needs) by exporting some of its products. This shows that domestic industries are completely dependent on the oil income for their import requirements and it is certain that after the exhaustion of oil reserves, they will face great perplexities.

Because of high protection, lack of correct management and also the enjoyment of monopoly rights, the assembly industries are not in healthy condition and the prices of their products are very high, and of low quality. On the whole, it seems that the protection of domestic industries in the past had been excessive and this caused the establishment of some unhealthy industries in the country unable to stand on their own feet without the help of the government. Probably during the first stage of industrialization, this policy was unavoidable, but in the future, it is necessary to change the protection policy and eliminate monopoly rights in order to create more competition between domestic and foreign goods, so that the assembly plants during a reasonable period can be transformed into real industries, to be able to provide their exchange expenses by exporting their products, and when the oil income comes to an end, the country could have some healthy and necessary industries to replace the oil industry.

In the last ten years, the government has made efforts to exempt taxes and grant subsidies, tempting to standarize export commodities to increase exports, but the result has not been remarkable and the exports have not increased parallel to imports. The exports of industrial products that previously were non-existent in 1973, comprised 25% of the total exports.

One of the unfavorable developments in 1961, was the very slow growth rate of agriculture in comparison to other sectors of the economy of the country, because of the rapid increase of the population and the rise of per capita income demand increasing enormously in Iran. This was one of the important factors causing a sharp rise of prices, especially food and raw material prices. The agricultural sector in earlier years, had been the net exporter, in recent years, it has been the net importer. For example, in 1962, the net balance of exports and imports of agricultural products was 279 million rials in surplus, but in 1972, it was about 8535 million rials in deficit and this deficit is growing every year.

There exists a dilemma in the government's foreign trade policy: on one hand, the government pursues the free trade policy to provide commodities in order to meet domestic demand and combat inflation, and on the other hand, it favors the protection policy in order to protect domestic industries and agriculture. In the early 1970's, the government had a protection policy, but in the last five years, it was forced to facilitate the imports of consumption goods in order to remove the shortage of those goods and by subsidizing agricultural products imported from foreign countries, it decreased agricultural production at home and this has been one of the causes of immense immigration of peasants to the towns.

To rectify this situation, the government of Iran should combat inflation by implementing other policies, other than the foreign trade policy. It should adopt a financial and monetary policy and abstain from carrying out ambitious projects. Furthermore, the government should support agricultural producers and consumers alike.

CHAPTER 9

SOCIAL CONDITIONS IN IRAN

At the beginning of this century, Iran was an agriculturally backward country and it's central government was very weak. Furthermore, it had been for more than a century under influence of both Russian and British powers, hence, during this period, Iran did not enjoy complete political and economic independence.

Under Pahlavi's regime, although Iran was politically and economically dependent on western countries, it had such a strong central government and a strong army, that was not imaginable 75 years before. In recent years, Iran had a major role in the Persian Gulf affairs and had become a second ranking power among the nations of the world, comparable to India in international affairs.

Iran is a country of 627,000 square miles, over five times the size of Britain. Its largest borders are with Russia on the north and Iraq on the west, it's northwest border is with Turkey and Afghanistan. It has frontiers on the west with Iraq, and on the east and southeast with Pakistan. The Persian Gulf stretches along it's southern border. Nearly 50% of the total land area of Iran is desert. Desert and mountain ranges separates the population centers from each other, and the main population resides in about 15% of the total area. The concentrations of the people are distributed around the western, southern and northern edges of the country.

In the past, because of the weakness of Iran's central government and lack of roads, different centers of the population had little contact with one another, and it is only in recent decades that a unified administration and unified communications were imposed on the country.

The population of Iran has increased from 10 million in 1900 to 14.6 million in 1940 and 33.6 million in 1976 and today it is nearly 40 million.

Until 1936, about 80% of the population was living in rural areas and 20% in towns, but at the present, more than 50% of the population is living in urban areas.

Structure of Iran's society

Iranian society has three main demographic features: First, as a result of the geographic character of the country, population density is very uneven in different areas. The greatest concentration is in the central province that includes Tehran. In 1976, this accounted for about 7 million or about a fifth of the total population. No other city rivals Tehran in population or importance. Villages and towns are very much dispersed and the distance between them is very large. Apart from the central province, the most populated provinces are those in the north, where sufficient rainfall supports the rich agriculture in the country. Khosistan is also one of the densely populated areas because of having the oil industry.

Table 16: Cities of over a quarter million inhabitants in 1976

Tehran	4,496,159
Isphahan	671,000
Mashad	670,180
Tabriz	598,576
Shiraz	414,408
Ahvaz	329,081
Abadan	296,081
Kermanshah	290,861

Source:
Iran Dictatorship and Development,

Fred Haliday

Half of the country has a population density of less than five persons per square mile. Consequently, Iran in comparison with other middle east countries, is considered densely populated, but in comparison with other third world countries like India, it is less populated. The second feature of Iranian society, is the presence of a nomadic population in Iran, and most of them speak languages other than the Persian language. In 1800 up to 50% of the population had been nomadic and in 1900 a third of it. Since Pahlavi's regime came to power, the government had tried to settle nomads in towns and consequently, their number had decreased considerably and in 1976, only six percent of the population (about 2 million) were nomads.

A third very important feature of Iranian society, is the linguistic and ethnic diversity of the country. The official and literary language of the country is Persian, spoken by about half of the population. Turkish is the second ranked language of 25% of the people, followed by Kurdish, Gilani, Beloutchi, and Turkman. There are Armenians and Assurins who speak their own languages.

Table 17: Linguistic groupings in Iranian society

language	percentage	language	percentage
Persian	50.2	Baluchi	2.3
Azerbaijani	20.6	Arabic	2.0
Gilani	6.1	Turkomeni	1.7
Luri-Bakhtiari	5.7	Armenian	0.6
Kurdish	5.6	Assyrian	0.4
Mazandarani	4.9		

Source: Iran Dictatorship and Development, Fred Haliday

Before Pahlavi's regime, the health condition of the people was in a deplorable state, and often, epidemic diseases such as colera and malaria were spreading over the country killing a great number of people. This was one of the important factors that prevented the increase of the population. During this period, illiteracy was common and there was no modern school or university in the country.

The economic development in Iran in recent decades has been accompanied by definite improvements in health and education, but still half of the population living outside the urban areas have not been affected by these changes.

In response to the improved economic and health conditions, the population growth rate has risen from 0.50 in 1930-1920 to 3.2 in the 1970's. The 1976 census showed that 53% of all Iranians are under the age of 20. There has been a great expansion in Iran's school and university system. Literacy has risen from 5% in 1900 to 15% in 1956 and 35% in the 1970's. More than 50% of population especially in the rural areas are illiterate. The university system that did not exist before Pahlavi's regime, has expanded greatly by establishing universities in all of the important cities of the country and by sending students to foreign countries. The number of university students in the country has increased from 25000 in 1965 to 170,000 in 1977 and in this year, about 55,000 students are studying in various fields of science in foreign countries.

Various classes of Iranian society

In 1900, a great majority of active people of the country (about 90%) were either in agriculture or in the nomadic sector, and there was no industry and the remaining 10% were in a handicraft trade or services.

The dominant classes of society in this period consisted of: the tribal leaders, land owners, merchants and aristocrats in the court and high officials of civil servants. Most of the land owners were living in towns, and this pattern had not changed until 1941.

Since the 1940's, there has been considerable changes in Iranian society, that may be summarized as follows:

1- There has been a decline in the position of tribal leaders, landowners, and religious leaders as a result of the land reform program and the power of government increased at the village level.

2- There has been an expansion in the number of farmers having enough land for themselves and in the number of land-less wage earning laborers. About 30% of those economically active are still working in agriculture.

3- With the expansion of the banking system, other state credit institutions and a modern commercial sector, there has been some decline in the power of the Iranian society but it still controls one third of the imports and two thirds of the retail businesses.

4- Emigration of the rural population to towns and the expansion of employment opportunities in towns created in the country a vast non-agricultural wage earning class. In 1977, there were 2.5 million people employed in manufacturing, and one million in construction out of a total of 10.4 million active population.

5- The government having at its disposal an ever increasing oil income, has become the dominant force in the economy and the most important employer in the country. In 1977 about 350,000 people were in the army and 800,000 in civil services out of them 160,000 were in education. Furthermore, around 1.5 million were employed in government industrial, or financial companies that were created by the participation of government.

6- The composition of new ruling class reflects the above economic changes: The new Iranian dominant classes comprises the upper ranks of the armed forces, high officials of civil servants, the rich capitalist landowners, financiers, entrpreneurs, and industrialists that have benefited from the oil income. Ten percent of the population that constitute the dominant classes appropriated for themselves 40% of the national income, and a small number of Iranian capitalists cooperate with the government in industry, commerce and agriculture.

7- Between the new ruling class and the growing number of wage laborers in towns and in the countryside, there exists a new intermediate class comprising of rich farmers owning land and employees in distribution, trade, professionals skilled in labor and others in the service sector; and the number of this class is growing.

The composition and orientation of the classes in Iran is of great importance for the outcome of the conflict between the dominant and the wage earning classes.

In the upcoming chapters, we will discuss in more detail, the changes in the class character of the Iranian society in the light of the growth of the state, the land reform, the industrial development and the growth of the size of the Iranian workers.

The role of women in the Iranian society

In the past, women in Iran were active economically in agriculture, nomadic activities and handicrafts, especially in the carpet weaving industry. But as the income of the farmers rose, there has been some decline in the rate of rural female economic activity outside the home. Husbands usually prefer their wives to stay at home and not work. In 1970, there was a rise in the level of female employment in the towns to 11% of the total employment. The percentage of female employment in Iran in comparison with other third world countries is generally low, but in comparison to other muslim countries, it is very high.

Women are in many respects in an inferior position to men. Female illiteracy is about 20% higher than that of men. In the past, the gap between men's illiteracy and that of the women was larger, but during Pahlavi's regime, it was gradually closing. Also, women are employed mostly in jobs that need less skill and therefore, their pay is much lower and far less for those women in the countryside.

As a result of the economic changes and approval of the family protection act in 1967, and it's implementation, the social conditions of women have improved greatly, especially in the towns. The muslim system of polygamy under which a man can have four wives is legal, but according to the family protection law, a wife must give her written consent in order for her husband to be able to take a second wife . Consequently polygamy has sharply declined. A great majority of marriages are at the present monogamous. The law also imposed a minimum age for marriage: 15 years for girls and 18 years for boys. Temporary marriage (Siegeh) in which a man can take a woman for a limited period as a wife is banned. This practice was a form of legalized prostitution, although Mullahs still sanction it in rural areas and small towns.

In towns, Iranian males have tried to adopt the sexual freer practices of the western countries, but Iranian women are prevented from doing so. Iranian women are controlled by their husbands, parents and even other relatives. Virginity in women is still highly valued, and those women who disregard the prevailing norms of ethics are severely punished. A dual standard therefore operates between men and women. Women have been allowed only to imitate western consumption patterns.

The government considers itself as the champion of women, but as with the land reform, and official trade unions, the changes are mostly superficial and designed to prevent any independent radical movement. Undoubtedly, the family protection act was a positive step in improving women's position and to some extent, it has been successful in preventing the worst abuses of the pre-existing system, but still, men and women are unequal in family and economic conditions. The predominant attitude of Iranian men towards their women is one of control and superiority.

The government introduced a population policy designed to reduce the birth rate from 3.2 to 2.4% and established a network of family planning clinics. Because of the unavailability and unacceptance of contraception especially among the poorer sector of urban and rural areas, this program has not been successful.

The role of religion in the Iranian society

A significant area of social life of the Iranians that the government has not been able to control is religion. Since the 16th century, as a result of Safavi Dynasty efforts, a sect of Islam called Shiet became the official religion on Iran, and 75% of the people of the country are followers of the twelve Imam branch of Shiet. Pahlavi's regime deprived the mullahs of the three main privileges that they enjoyed previously, land owning, practicing judgement, law and finally education.

Throughout the 1970's, there has been a rise in religious activity. The mullahs opposed the western values in conjunction with the economic development in the country, and they were against social changes through mosque as the only institution in Iran completely independent of the state.

The boom of the oil income and economic progress promoted the religious institutions, for example, the number of pilgrims visiting the holy city of Meshad has increased from 332,00 in 1966 to 3.5 million in 1976, and bazaar merchants who financially sustained the mullahs paid religious institutions and religious leaders in Azkat (religious tax) more than taxes to the state.

There are about 80,000 mosques and 1200 holy shrines that have become centers for resistance and opposition to the government policies. It is estimated that there are about 180,000 mullahs in Iran that help religious authorities in opposing governmental policies. Furthermore, in 1778, there were about 10,000 religious students studying religious matters in Gom and Meshad to become future mullahs, with a five million dollar annual budget. In addition, there are about 10,000 shrine attendants of which half live in Tehran.

With the growing popular opposition against the regime's social and political policies, after the year 1973, mosques became centers of opposition, and they were the only institution that were able to support the popular discontent in a situation that every kind of political activity was prohibited. Through the mosques were organized vast manifestations of protest that ended in the recent revolution.

The discussion in this chapter shows that efforts of government to establish in the country a unified policy and culture have not been successful and on the contrary, social and economic changes created conflicts between old and new values and cultures and between ethnic minorities and the working ruling class.

CHAPTER 10

WORKING CLASS IN IRAN

In Iran, as in most countries, because of the economic development, a considerable number of the population shifted from agricultural to non-agricultural activities. At the beginning of this century, 90% of the labor force in Iran was working in the countryside, but in 1946, the workin force in the rural areas had fallen to 75% and in 1966 to 47% and in 1977 to 33%.

In 1977, out of 10.6 million of the working force in the country, around 6.8 million were working in the non-agricultural sector of which 2.5 million were employed in industrial activities.

The majority of the economically active population of the country is now in one form or another wage-earners, and a new important social force has been created in Iran. Yet, despite it's growing number, since the coup of the 28th of Mordad in 1953, independent activity of workers to form unions or syndicates was prevented. But it seems that this situation is unlikely to continue in the future, as the increase of strikes after 1973 shows that there will be resistance to government. It is certain that the working classes wish to have independent expression is very strong, and they will play an important role in the country's politics in the future.

In the following analysis, we are going to study briefly the main characteristics of the working class in Iran and it's role in the country's politics.

In Iran, as in other third world countries, because of the existence of various forms of employment, a small number of the working force is only employed in modern industries, and because of ethnic and linguistic differences, it is difficult to consider all of the working force of the country as a unified political framework.

The growth of the working class- The growth of the number of working class in Iran is, above all, the result of the economic development of the country. Before the second world war, the only important industrial activity of the country was oil, and the real industrialization of the country began in the 1950's. Since then, employment in the oil industry has be stagnant, but employment in manufacturing, and construction has increased substantially. Although oil is very important from an economic development point of view, it has no significant role in employment. Employment in the oil industry during the period under review has always been less than 1% of the working force of the country, while employment in industry and construction has tripled during the last twenty years.

There is also great differences in wages between workers that work in modern industries and those in small industries and in handicrafts. In Iran, in comparison with other developing countries, a higher percentage of the working force is employed in manufacturing activity.

Table 18: Employed population by major sectors and labor force (in thousands)

sector	annual totals				increases
	1956	1966	1972	1977	1972-1977
agriculture	3326	3774	3800	3800	0
oil	25	26	40	55	15
mining and manuf. (incld. hdcfts.)	816	1324	1820	2500	680
construction	336	520	710	980	270
utilities	12	53	60	65	5
commerce	355	513	650	725	75
transp. & comunic.	208	224	255	280	25
govern. services	248	474	640	780	140
bank & other serv.	582	650	900	1040	140
Total employed	5908	7558	8875	10225	1350
unemployed	158	284	320	375	55
Total lab. force	6066	7842	9195	10600	1405

Source: Employment and income policy of Iran, I.L.O. 1973

Iran's working force is concentrated mostly in specific industrial centers. In 1973, around 48.7% of them were working in the Tehran area, 7.8% in Isphahan, 6.9% in Tabriz, 6.6% in Khosistan and the remaining in other areas.

The three main economic sectors of wage earning activity in the country are: oil, manufacturing and construction that will be discussed in that order.

Workers in the oil industry

In 1920, about 20,000 workers were employed in the oil industry, it had increased in 1951 to 55,000 and also in this year, about 1500 workers were working for contractors of the oil industry.

As a result of the oil industry boom, and the increase of employees and workers, the town of Abadan, site of the great refinery, grew from a small fishing village to a big city, so that it is called in Iran the second London, where the whole population depended directly or indirectly on it's employment in the oil industry.

At the beginning, most of the skilled workers were indians but later when Iranian workers were trained, they were replaced by Iranians. Despite the intensive capital nature of the industry, a large proportion of workers are unskilled because production and the refining processes are so automated that only a small number of skilled workers are required. Because of automation, the absolute number of workers employed in the oil industry has decreased in recent years. In 1975, the number of workers in the oil industry was 45,000, nearly the same as 20 years before, but per capita output has increased more than 20 times. Therefore, we can conclude that the main features of the oil industry are as follows: the oil industry creates a small number of employment opportunities in underdeveloped countries, and it has few linkages with the local economy, but it creates great opportunities for employment indirectly through investment of it's income.

Working force in the manufacturing industry

According to statistics published by I.L.O., the number of workers in the manufacturing industries in Iran has increased greatly in the last 20 years. During 1972-1977, the employment in the manufacturing industries increased about 680,000 of which 580,000 were employed in various industries and the remaining one hundred thousand were self-employed. There is no doubt that after the increase of the oil income, employment in industries increased more rapidly.

Table 19: Indication of wages and employment in selected industries (100" 1969-70)

industries	wages 1974-5	employ 74-5
total selected industries	292.2	140.4
of which:		
tobacco	221.8	111.5
spinning and textiles	274.3	121.4
leather	219.4	98.0
machine made shoes	297.4	168.5
petrochemicals	402.8	242.3
pharmaceuticals	282.1	173.2
cement	283.6	148.0
basic metals	349.8	195.8
household appliances (electrical and non-electrical)	272.9	136.8
radio, t.v. telephone	377.1	226.8
electrical tools	352.9	217.0
motor vehicles	368.8	170.1
sheet glass	562.5	325.9

Source: Bank Markazi annual report 1975-6

There are great differences among the workers of the manufacturing industries: First, 20% of them are self-employed, therefore, they are not workers in any strict sense of this term. Second, the majority of industries are small units employing less than 10 persons. In 1972, out of a total of 225,000 firms, 219,000 were small units and in that year, 72% of the 2.5 million labor force were employed in small units, and usually they had less skills, and their wages were low. Wages in modern industries are generally twice as much as in traditional ones.

The working force in construction

Most emmigrants from other countries are employed in construction fields, and usually, employment for them is temporary and seasonal. It is very common in underdeveloped countries like Iran, that the first employment a peasant procures upon coming to a town is in construcion, but usually he moves after awhile to other fields of activity.

In Iran, like in the other countries, construction workers are mostly comprised of peasants. After the increase of the oil income, employment in construction rose from 336,000 in 1956 to 900,000 in 1977. Within the construction labor force, the difference of wages was very great and sometimes the skilled laborer as the plumbers, electricians, and carpenters receive 15 times more wages than unskilled ones.

Characteristics of the labor force in Iran

Many features of the labor force in Iran are similar to the features of workers of other developing countries, because most of those employed in industry are from a peasant background. According to the survey carried out by the government in 1963, 68.3% of all Tehran's factory workers had been born in villages. Only in the oil industry established a long time ago in the country were there workers that were born in the towns where they were working.

The other feature of the Iranian labor force is that a substantial part of the workers are working in villages at textile workshops. For example, 1.2 million workers are employed in the country in the textile and hand weaving carpet industries, of which 70% are working in villages that comprises 17% of the total working force of the country. Consequently, the labor in handicraft, is still an important factor in the country's employment situation.

One important feature of the Iranian working class formation is that, it is based on a massive and recent migration from rural areas to towns, especially to Tehran. In 1956, 31% of the population was urban, by 1976, it had risen to 47%. Tehran had received a disproportionate amount of these emigrants. Therefore it's population had increased during the decades of 1950 and 1960 at 5.5% yearly, and after 1973 it increased more than 8%. Tehran has today more than five million population and this creates major problems such as traffic, shortage of water, electricity and pollution of air in the capital of the country. The emigrant workers live usually in the south part of Tehran and there is such a great gap in the standard of living in the north and south of Tehran that seldom exists in capitals of other countries. Tehran with 5 million inhabitants still does not have a modern sewage system. The waste and polluted air are concentrated in the south of the city and endangers the health of its residents.

Unemployment in Iran- In the years immediately before the revolution, Iran had both a labor shortage and a labor surplus. The shortage was for skilled and managerial personnel, therefore, in 1976, there were about 50,000 foreign skilled laborers working in Iran. At the same time, there were unskilled people both literate and illiterate unemployed. In addition, there was a great number of disguised unemployed workers in government administrations and also in villages.

Wages- In Iran, the oil boom was accompanied by a considerable rise of wages in most fields of economic activities, but most of the skilled workers and government employees in new establishments benefited from it. On the contrary, unskilled workers and ordinary government employees because of rapid inflation (especially a great increase of cost of living) have not benefited from the increase of oil income, but their real income had deteriorated.

Women in the Iranian economy

The position of women in Iran has improved con-considerably in the last two decades. With the exception of a minority of educated and skilled women who work in towns, the majority of women workers that have less skill, receive less wages and work longer hours in comparison with men. Official statistics show that in 1972, 13% of all women over the age of 12 years (1.4 million) were employed, the comparable figure for men was around 68%, but this figure is misleading because it does not take into account women's work in villages and in homes. Women in villages and nomads work along side the men. In villages, about 72% of carpet and textile workers are women.

The illiteracy of women in the villages is about 90% much more than men, while in towns 30% of women are literate. 200,000 of the women in towns are working in different professions as: teaching, secretarial, medicine and etc.

Government policy regarding the workers

The government in implementing development programs is confronted with a dilemma. On one hand, this program needs the consent and cooperation of workers, on the other hand, because of the despotic and absolute nature of government, it denies any independent voice of the working class, therefore, the government makes efforts to attract cooperation and at the same time to control them. In 1960, in order to attract the cooperation of workers, the government established an insurance scheme, and since then, a number of measures have been approved and put into action by the government for the improvement of conditions of the working class.

The two important schemes are: the profit sharing scheme of 1963, and the workers share program of 1975, both being respectively, the sixth and thirteenth principles of the Shah's white revolution. The profit sharing scheme covers only the workers of firms having ten or more workers, but those working in the oil industry, railway and tobacco industries are excluded. Workers benefiting from this scheme receive up to 20% of the profits, and those profits are to be distributed according to seniority and wages. Most firms considered this as a threat to their position and by publishing incorrect accounts with less profit, they abstained from paying workers their fair shares and usually gave them one month extra salary instead of a part of the profits. This scheme had little effect in improving the position of the workers especially in enterprises that had less than ten workers.

In January 1970, the workers share scheme was introduced. It involved the sale of 49% of the firms shares to employees and workers of those firms. Only the companies covered themselves with this scheme, revealing that their minimum capital was to be 100 million rials or its fixed assets to be 200 million rials or more, or their yearly turn over to be a minimum of 250 million rials. The workers qualified to benefit from this scheme had been employed for three years in the company. In 1978, 320 enterprises were announced as being eligible for this purpose and the workers had a choice to receive loans with 4% interest and buy the shares. This scheme was also introduced to prevent the workers from moving rapidly from one industry to another, and to increase productivity of the labor force. This scheme was not successful.

The growth of the trade unions in Iran

Most of the time, the Iranian working class was denied any independent activity to form trade unions. Yet, it had some independent class activity to some degree in three periods. The first was 20 years before Reza Shah's coming to power, the second was in the period between 1945 and 1953 and the third was after 1973.

During the first period, since the number of workers in towns was very small and modern industry at that time was virtually non-existent, workers and employers formed unions in the form of guilds and their aim was mostly to oppose the import of goods similar to home produced goods, or they participated with other people in campaigns to establish a parlimentary government. The first workers union was formed in 1906 by workers of printing firms with the help and support of communism, but because they were weak and small in number, the union was not successful. From the beginning of Pahlavi's dynasty reign in 1928, all trade unions were banned.

The first comprehensive labor law in Iran was passed in 1936. This law contained only articles about working conditions in industrial firms with no mention of the right to strike or to form trade unions by the workers.

During the second world war, the country was occupied by foreign forces, as a consequence of worsening economic conditions in Iran, especially the inflation of more than 100% per year, discontent spread among the workers. In these circumstances, workers with the help of the Toudeh party (Communist party of Iran affiliated to Moscow) formed strong unions, and in 1944, the central council of the Iranian workers trade unions was created with more than 100,000 members and in that year, it joined the world's federation of workers unions. Between the year 1942 and 1946, workers' strikes were wide spread throughout the country.

After an attempt on the life of the Shah in 1949, by a member of the Toudeh party, that party was banned, and after 1953, the worker's right to strike was also legally abolished.

Official trade unions

As in Germany and Italy before the second world war, the Iranian government, in order to attract the cooperation of workers, on the basis of the labor law of 1959, created the official union of workers. The main functions of these unions were as follows: to conclude collective agreements with employers to purchase, sell and acquire movable and immovable property on conditions that it is not for commercial purposes, to defend the occupational rights and the interests of their members, to establish cooperatives to meet the requirements of their members and to establish unemployment funds for the purpose of assisting unemployed workers.

In this law, the right to strike was not mentioned and all kinds of political activity of workers through trade unions is prohibited. In reality, the unions were administered by Savak (secret police), and the representatives of Savak were present in all factories. The union only administered the welfare affairs of workers and when necessary by encouragement of Savak, they participated in the manifestations to support the regime.

CHAPTER 11

STATE AND ITS' ROLE IN ECONOMIC DEVELOPMENT

In all countries, the state is an institution that takes monopoly power in its hands and thereby establishes order, and enforces the law in the interest of those that the state represents. At the present, in nearly all societies, the states have more effective power that in the past, especially in the economic affairs of those societies. In capitalistic developing countries, because of the weakness of the bourgeois and middle classes, and the incompetence of domestic capitalists and entrepreneurs to initiate and implement infrastructural and industrial projects, the government's intervention in development activities has played a dominant role than in capitalistic developed countries.

In Iran, in addition to the above facts, the economic development is financed by the oil income, and the oil income belongs to the government, hence, intervention of the state in the economic field is prominent. In Iran, the government decides how the oil is to be allocated for various uses, what projects and which groups would benefit from governmental investment funds. Therefore, the analysis of economic transformation in Iran requires understanding the form of the state and what social groups interests it represents.

During Pahlavi's regime, the country was governed by one person in charged, namely the Shah. It is evident that one man alone can not rule 35 million people, therefore, the question arises, what classes collaborate with the state and which state represents which groups and classes. It is also important to know why the political system of Iran has taken the shape of a monarchist dictatorship.

One important feature of Iran's recent development is that is has been shaped by international ties with more advanced capitalistic economies through the sale of oil, foreign investment, technology and thereby has become dependent on the economies of the western capitalistic countries. Iran, since the second world war, in political and military spheres has allied with the United States of America. Some people exaggerate in regards to foreign influences in Iran. In fact, Mohammad Reza Shah was not as independent as he himself claimed, nor as reliant as most of his opponents alleged.

We are going to discuss first, the historical formation of the Iranian state, and then, its contemporary characteristics.

The historical transformation of the Iranian state

The Iranian state has been the product of some major events in this century and each of them had some effects at it's formation.

The first event was the constitutional revolution 1905-11. This was an effort by merchants and intellectuals in the towns to limit the power of kings and to establish a parlimentary system. Since the late 18th century, Iran was ruled by Kajar dynasty. During this period, although Iran was not a colony, the central government by it's capacity to administer the provinces outside of Tehran, gradually became very weak, and the influences of foreign powers, as we have shown in earlier chapters, in

Iran's internal affairs increased. They acquired privileges that were detrimental to the economic independence of the country, and so the progress of the country in economic and industrial fields was prevented.

In 1891, a major national movement developed in protest against the granting of a tobacco monopoly to a British company, and this movement supported by religious leaders remained strong until it ended in constitutional revolution. There is much dispute about the causes of this revolution, but what is important is that, this event was the first in Iranian history in which an attempt was made to limit the power of the Shah and transfer the law making power to the peoples' elected representatives.

The constitutional revolution failed to bring about any fundamental changes in the class situation in Iran, and in fact, the ruling old classes again had the power of government in their hands, because the forces against Quajar kings were weak and were confined to some cities as Tehran, Tabriz and also Tsarist,Russia was supporting them. During the first world war, both British and Russian as well as Turkish armies invaded Iran and the Russian revolution in 1917 removed the Quajar's main patron.

In 1919, there was no strong central government and in Khorasan, Gilan and Khosistan, separatist movements were in power. At this time, the only coherent military force was a unit comprised of 3000 men that was established by Russian Cossak officers in 1879.

In 1921, Reza Khan, the leader of this unit, by British encouragement, staged a bloodless coup and became prime minister of war and later prime minister of Iran. Within a year, Reza Khan became a prominent political leader of the country and in 1925, by approval of the parliment, Ahmad Shah was deposed and Reza Khan became king and so the Pahlavi dynasty was founded.

Reza Khan created the first strong central government in Iran. He built a modern army and crushed all separatist movements. He established the first ministerial system, developed educational, health and transport systems. After 1934, he began to encourage a small industrialization program, but he did not introduce land reform. Reza Khan's rule was terminated by outside military intervention.

In Shahrivar 1941, ally armies invaded Iran and the country was occupied by their forces. Reza Shah was forced to abdicate and to go into exile. His son Mohammad Reza replaced him as Shah of Iran. Temporarily, the dictatorial government was transformed to a democratic government. Liberties not enjoyed since the days when the constitution was restored, freedom of workers to establish independent unions, formation of parties, and the freedom of the press was established in the country. At the end of the war, two independent governments, one in Kurdistan and the other in Azarbaydjan were formed with the aid of the Soviet army. Later, the central government with the support of the United States succeeded to establish it's control over the provinces, and the Toudeh party that openly supported sepratist movements was discredited among the people.

In 1951, under the leadership of Dr. Mossadegh, the oil industry was nationalized and another crises developed in the country. Soon Mossadegh's government was in direct conflict with the Shah, and Shah's power was curtailed by pro-Mossadegh elements in parliament and at the end, the Shah was forced to leave the country.

In 1952, the government of Mossadegh was ousted by a coalition of internal and external forces. The United States government, feared that Mossadeghs' policies would result in communists taking over the country. This helped opposition groups in Iran to overthrow Mossadegh's government. Opponents of the Shah exaggerated the role of the American government in overthrowing Mossadegh. In fact, internal factors in this event were more instrumental, because Mossadegh did not succeed in establishing stability in the country, in addition, the ruling class in Iran was against him. Later as a result of deterioration in the economic conditions of the country, his popularity also declined. He had no definite economic program to replace the stoppage of the oil income. Religious leaders that in the first year of Mossadegh's government supported him, later joined his opponents.

Since 1953, the Shah was able to strengthen his power throughout Iran, he abolished all legal and institutional freedoms. In the years 1960-63, the government was faced with another crisis. The Iranian economy had been in recession since 1958, the budget showed a deficit and the balance of payment was in disequilibrium. The Shah with encouragement from President Kennedy of the United States of America, proclaimed a program of reforms under the name of the white revolution, and also to disarm his critics and opponents. These programs included:

land reform, universal education, granting the right to elect or to be elected to women, etc. But he did not permit free election fearing that would weaken his power. He even dismissed the prime minister, Dr. Ali Amini, who was acting too independently to some extent.

In 1963, there was an uprise in Tehran and in some other cities led by some Mullahs and the Shah crushed it by his army. It is believed that several thousand people were killed on this occasion. But until the late 1970's, the regime took the initiative and the rise of the oil income gave an additional impact to the economic development of Iran. Also in the past, most of the time, the protest of the people had taken the shape of religion, Islam, which aided the government at times, and in other times opposed the power of government.

There has never been a colony in Iran, classes before capitalism lasted longer than in other third world countries. During Reza Shah's reign, although some social changes occurred in Iran, for a long period, the majority of the people were employed in agriculture and only after land reform and carrying out economic plans was the capitalistic regime established in the country.

The importance of Iran for world powers is in its strategic position that separates Russian from the Persian Gulf. In the nineteenth century, it was important for Britain to be a neighbor to India, but today, the oil of the Persian Gulf has more importance to western countries, in case an anti-capitalistic regime comes to power in Iran that would have a great effect on all countries of the area.

Historically, Iran was governed always by despotic , after the revolution, the weak bourgeois class did not succeed in establishing democracy in the country. Until 1960, the bourgeois sect was weak and the government having at it's disposal a vast amount of oil income everday grew economically and socially stronger.

General characteristics of the Iranian state

Most features of the Iranian state to a greater or lesser degree are found in other third world countries, and the specific form that each takes in Iran combine together and makes the Iranian state of the 1970's. These features are as follows:

The first feature is that the Iranian state is a capitalistic one, i.e., factors of production (land, goods, labor, capital) belongs to private persons, goods can be sold and bought on the market. The state also plays an active role in production and distribution and mostly protects the interest of the capitalists. At the same time, because of the great role of government in economics, a large bureaucratic governmental class is created, although its members do not own factors of production directly, but the upper sections of the state apparatus benefit from the economic surplus extracted. Generally speaking, the bureaucratic class, private capitalists and high army officers form together the ruling class of the country and play a dominant role in running the economic and social affairs of the country. To make a just and realistic judgment about benefits of the economic development of Iran, we have to take into consideration the different classes of society and show which of them benefit from it.

After 1950, the middle class in Iran increased considerably. Opponents of the regime especially the communists denied totally the progress of Iran and claimed that the situation was better before. They condemned the regime and called it fascist or dependent on western capitalism without taking into account the real facts. But in Iran, although the government protects the interest of the bourgeois, it is not directly dependent and responsible to it and even often chooses policies against the interests of the capitalist and bourgeois classes, and, in the past, has favored low income groups, especially workers. There is no doubt that the economic development caused the wealth of the country to be centralized in the hands of a minority of special groups that consisted of landowners, a higher stratum of bourgeois and owners of industrial and financial institutions. Consequently, 10% of the people now are consuming 40% of the national income and so the gap between the rich and poor has widened.

The second characteristic of the Iranian state is, the country is a developing one and the government is the main stimulant of development. The main object of the Shah's white revolution was to create a favorable environment for economic development that includes: land reform, nationalization of forests, selling government industries to private persons, the right of women to elect or to be elected, participation of workers in profits of industrial firms, development of health services and universal education. In reality, the white revolution was not a real revolution but a kind of reform to prevent a geniune revolution and also to strengthen the power of the king.

The third feature of Iranian characteristics is the form of dictatorship. At that time, this was the only kind of state that could establish stability for investment and carrying out reforms. The Shah extended it's dictatorship and control to all aspects of the political and social life of the people, so that in the 1970's, all unions, newspapers, and parliment was a fabrication of the state and the people had no voice in them. Dictatorship in Iran was neither an army nor group dictatorship. It was a dictatorship of only one person. The Shah usually dismissed any individual from government that acquired popularity and by creating enmity and conflict between the ruling class and censorship controlled in all institutions of the country. Consequently, this policy, enable no one to have any kind of initiative and all government officials in order to gain maximum material benefits tried to conform themselves to the regime, and as a result of this, corruption spread all over the country. The corruption of government's high officials was in the form of participation in contracts of industrial firms or having shares in their profits and also to receive bribe or commission from government contracts. Relatives of the Shah and most of the officials of court had dealings in most of the industrial firms or in contracts that those firms made with the government, and their participation was sometimes through the

Pahlavi Foundation, especially in banks, hotels, casinos and factories. On the whole, in the Pahlavi regime, the people were attracted to support the government for material benefits instead of ideology. There is no doubt that the main part of the social and political difficulties and shortcomings of the regime were due to the historical background of Iranian characteristics. At the same time, it is clear that the Shah after 1960 was such a meganom that was not able to accept advice from anybody and was choosing for members of government and electing for parliment and high officials of the army, those people that accepted wholeheartedly his decisions and were yes men.

In the last 20 years, there has been a vast attempt to arouse nationalism spirited together with the belief that only kings created the greatness of Iran in the past. Eminent efforts of this kind was the extravagant celebration of 2500 anniversary in the establishment of the kingdom of Iran. Or course, there was great publicity regarding the greatness of Iran before Arab invasion to Iran and the government was making all kinds of efforts to create close ties between nationalism and the kingdom.

Another feature of Iran's regime in recent years was it's dependence on the United States. This country in the past has helped Iran to keep it's territory unified against Russia, that was supporting separatist movements in the events of Azarbaydjan and Kordistan and also helped the regime oust the Mossadegh government. After 1946, the state of Iran had become politically, militarily and economically dependent on western advanced countries. Most of the arms, technology and training of personnel was provided by the United States. In fact, this dependence was not complete and some times there was a difference of opinion between the Shah and the western countries, in determining the oil price of the OPEC countries. The Shah was supporting sharp increases of oil against the interests of the western countries.

CHAPTER 12

SUCCESSES AND SHORTCOMINGS OF ECONOMIC DEVELOPMENT PLANS

As shown in previous chapters during Pahlavi's regime, especially after the year of 1960, the Iranian economy achieved great progress by carrying out five economic development plans and according to the national income indexes, the country enjoyed a high growth rate in most sectors of it's economy. The gross national product of the country increased an average of 10% per year, and per capita income of the people rose from 200 dollars in 1962 to around 2000 dollars in 1976. During this period many important roads, ports and airports were constructed. Also, many multipurpose dams were built to produce electricity, and store water for irrigation. Most towns were provided with electricity and healthy water that before was non-existent.

Production of oil increased to more than 5 million barrels a day, and the Iranian national oil company expanded it's activity enormously in the country and also abroad, and so it became one of the most important oil companies in the world. The gas that previously was burning in flames, and wasted was exploited for exporting, injection into oil wells and used as raw material for petrochemical industries. Furthermore, thousand of basic and consumer industries were established in the country.

On the whole, there is no doubt that Iran in the last 20 years enjoyed one of the highest rates of economic growth among third world capitalist or communist countries.

Notwithstanding the brilliant achievements, the economy of the country suffered some shortcomings and weaknesses that we are going to discuss in this chapter.

Unhealthy and unbalanced economic growth with unfavorable infrastructure- Economic development in European countries began in the 18th century by way of the industrial revolution, that was simultaneous with social and agricultural transformation. In these countires, during this period, fundamental changes occurred in cultural, political and social fields that created favorable infrastructure for industrial and agricultural development.

In the early years of the 19th century, a special kind of division of labor came to existence between the countries that had experienced industrial revolution and the other countries. For example, the European countries were producing industrial products and the undeveloped countries, raw materials, and agricultural products. The trade between the two groups of countries expanded on the basis of this kind of division of labor, and so the economies of the two types of countries were complementary to each other.

As a result of the first world war, as well as the great economic depression of 1930, there came important changes in the above mentioned relations between the countries. The undeveloped countries began to produce some of the goods that they imported previously from abroad and industrial countries produced some artificial material to replace previously imported ones, and at the same time, by way of increasing productivity and producing cheaper and better quality products, they succeeded to expand their export of industrial goods. The underdeveloped countries, contrary to industrial countries, with the help of government (imposing heavy duties on imports and vast financial aid) created some comsumer industries on an unfavorable social infrastructure. As distribution of wealth and income was very unequaled in these countries. Only a minority group of people in towns had sufficient purchasing power to buy industrial products, therefore, small units of industries were established to satisfy the demand of those groups. There was no specialization and standardization in the industries of these countries and as a result of it, underdeveloped countries established small units of consumer industries that were mostly unhealthy and were able to survive only with the help of governments. Also, these governments by enormous investments directly created some basic industries, as iron mill, petrochemical, electricity, etc. In these countries, these industries were used as subsidies to those consumer industries that produced goods for rich groups of people living in towns; for example, expansion of electric production helped the production of consumer luxury goods as electric appliance, and residential buildings in towns. While enduring healthy and steady economic development, it was necessary that those basic industries be used as support for agricultural, mining and machine tool industries.

In Iran, like most other underdeveloped countries, industrialization followed the existing demand and as a result of it, the gap between the rich and poor widened. Foreign factors were also effective in fixing the direction of economic development, and production of luxury goods was encouraged by them. Generally speaking, it can be said, the conditions of social structure and existing demand together with foreign factors determined the direction of industrialization in Iran.

To achieve industrialization in Iran, there was a need for more skilled labor and personnel, machine tools, raw materials and marketing . As domestic conditions became unfavorable, it was difficult if not impossible to produce them at home, and so government began to import all of them from foreign countries. Therefore, as a result of industrialization, the country became economically more dependent on other countries instead of being more self sufficient. The integration of the economy of Iran with the economical aspects of other industrial capitalist countries was accomplished through multinational companies, most of them being American companies. These companies established branches in Iran and in other underdeveloped countries, participated in investments with internal capitalists or sold patent rights and used imported machine tools, technology and foreign management, and produced consumer goods similar to those consumed in western countries, especially the United States, for the upper classes of the society.

As a result of this new kind of international division of labor, that usually is called Neocolonialism, the imports of underdeveloped countries increased much more than their exports and therefore, their balance of payment was impaired. After a short period because of the shortage of foreign exchanges, their growth stopped. Certainly, the countries like Iran that enjoyed an enormous oil income for a longer time would be able to finance its imports, but after exhaustion of the oil reserves, Iran would encounter greater difficulties in balancing their internal and external economy.

Furthermore, because of the concentration of ownership of industries in the hands of a small group of individuals, a minority of capitalist reaped all the fruits of the economic development, but the majority of people of the country are deprived from the benefits of it.

The other important problem in Iran was that the supply of agriculture is very low and therefore, because of the rapid increase of population and rising demand for food and raw materials, the prices rose more than the increase of the income of low income groups. This factor was also effective in widening the gap between the rich and the poor. Also, as a result of stagnant agriculture, a considerable number of peasants emigrated to towns especially Tehran and created great difficulties for government from the point of view of employment, housing, water, and electricity.

In Iran, like in other underdeveloped countries, private capitalists were not prepared to invest in new projects that require vast amounts of investments and were risky; the government undertook those projects and created enormous bureaucracy. The governmental institutions were old and lacked skills and were usually corrupt, therefore a considerable amount of the countries resources were wasted.

Some economists believe that unfavorable side-effects of the economic development in the third world countries like Iran, namely, internal and external unbalance, foreign dependence and the existence of a dual economy, are the result of the first stage of economic development and at later stages,it would be eliminated automatically, but as we have shown, these undesirable features are the result of an existing structure of society. As long as the social, administrative and economic framework of these countries is not changed, these difficulties would not be solved.

Undoubtedly, foreign factors had great effects in the direction the economic development took in these countries, but this must not cause us to undermine internal factors. We can conclude that different and complex foreign and internal factors created a framework in which to operate the system. The foreign factors, comprised of all institutions that have come to existence as a result of economic, political and cultural connections of the country. With these dominant foreign centers, the internal factors consisted of natural resources, political ideologies, social institutions of the country, policies and attitudes of government, social groups and last but not least the moral concepts and characters of the people of the country.

In summary, the features of economic development of underdeveloped countries such as in Iran in the framework of the existing system are as follows: Integration of the economy of these countries to the economy of industrial capitalist countries has made them, economically, politically and culturally more dependent on capitalist countries. Usually the exports of these countries comprise of a few items of raw material and agricultural products that are very sensitive to price changes and have a weak position in international markets. In addition, mostly foreigners control the production and marketing of their resources and these countries have to import technology, capital goods and management from abroad. Usually, there are two separate sections in the econonmy of these countries, one modern and foreign oriented economy in big cities or around the important resources like oil that operates with a capital intensive technology, foreign skills and management, and the other traditional economy that operates with the pre-Newtonian technology. There are two different kinds of culture to match the dualism economy, tradition and consumption habits in each of the two sections of society. Hence, it is clear that development has transformed in these countries especially in Iran, once coherent society into two seprate societies, each of them being like one separate nation with a different economy, culture, traditions and way of life.

In these countries before economic development, there has been a structure of classes and power that assembled in the hands of the minority groups. The development process not only had not eliminated those classes but also added bureaucrats and owners of industries to the ruling classes, along with landowners and merchants who all together make a new ruling class that enjoyed the fruits of development . The government protected their interests, but the majority of people that comprises the unskilled workers, peasants and governments ordinary employees do not benefit, and if so, they benefited very little from the results of economic development.

In Iran, the economic development under the existing system, has widened the gap between high income and low income groups, so that 5% of the people appropriate for themselves more than 30% of the national income . This is one of the important factors that intensified discontent among people and caused a revolution.

<u>The unbalanced economic development in Iran-</u>

The rapid economic growth in Iran has created disequilibrium among different sectors of the economy, different areas of the country, and different groups of people.

The principal part of it's growth is related to

the oil income and services, but agriculture and infrastructure facilities failed to develop parallel to other sectors of the economy. In 1962, the national income of the country consisted of 35% agriculture, 12% oil income, 13% services and 40% industry and mines. This changed in 1977 to 10% agriculture, 38% oil, 38% services and 16% mines and industry.

The above figures show everyday, the economy of Iran has become more dependent on the oil income and the real growth rate is much less than what the government claims. The government includes the oil income in the national income of the country, while it should be considered as capital, and later on, when the oil reserves are depleted, the country could stand on it's own feet. Furthermore, the injection of the enormous oil income in the economy of Iras has intensified inflation that in the long run is unfavorable to the economic development of the country.

Too much increase of services in recent years in Iran, also shows a vast extenstion of bureacracy and inflation of government employees, that most part of it is disguised unemployed and does not add to the supply of goods and real services ; it only adds to the demand for goods and real services and thus causes the increase of prices.

Agricultural stagnation in Iran caused the increase in food and agricultural raw material prices and made the country dependent for a long time on foreign countries in providing the food of the people and raw materials needed for the industries. Slow development of infrastructure facilities such as roads, ports, railroads, and electricity caused the government to pay enormous sums to shipowner companies to compensate the delay of unloading ships that sometimes took more than six months while some important projects remained unfinished.

The unbalanced development of different provinces of the country created dualism in the economy and society of the country and caused those provinces that are far away from the center to remain poor and backward.

Inequality of wealth and income was intensified by economic development and spread discontent all over the country finally ended in revolution.

Stagnation of agriculture

As previously discussed, land reform made some changes in ownership of land, but land was distributed unequally and a considerable number of peasants were deprived of having enough land for cultivation, and earning their livelihood, and thus two groups of farmers were created in villages, one group of rich farmers and bourgeois and the other group of proletarian peasants, poor without land. Furthermore, productivity of agricultural activity, because of not using modern methods of production and better seeds and fertilizer did not increased. The government also failed to put sufficient amounts of credit at the disposal of peasants, and the small amount of funds that were earmarked for agriculture was appropriated by rich peasants, who used it for unproductive ends, such as pilgrimages to holy shrines or marriage ceremonies and otherkinds of short term purposes. Cooperatives were established in villages but becasue of the lack of efficient management, they were not able to fulfill their duties. The big agricultural corporations as a result of incorrect planning were faced with failure.

Mechanization and transformation of farms to orchards caused the decrease of employment in the countryside, and so unemployed peasants were forced to emigrate to towns especially to Tehran and this created unemployment and other difficulties in the towns, and a vast amount of human resources of the country was wasted.

The growth rate of the agricultural sector during implementation of the third and fourth plan was much lower than the average rate of other sectors of the economy. Because of the increase of population yearly, at the rate of 3.5% and rising per capita income demand for agricultural products increased 12% per year, while agricultural output was increasing only 2% and government in order to meet the demand and prevent the increasing of food prices began to import a considerable amount of food from other countries and granted subsidies to imported products. This policy was also, one of the main factors that stagnated agricultural activity in the country.

Income of town workers that was at the beginning of the third plan, twice as much as the peasants, at the end of the fourth plan became eight times more. We can conclude, that agriculture in Iran remained backward and weak and the relation between agriculture and industry had not developed. In Iran, industries provided 30% of their raw materials from internal sources and the remaining from foreign sources and agriculture, obtained 15% of its needs from domestic industries and the rest from outside sources.

The private sector, because of agricultural production, to some extent, is conditioned by climatic elements in Iran. The farm units are very dispersed and there is no agricultural insurance scheme and no inclination to invest in this field. There is no doubt that until the government creates necessary facilities in order for agricultural activity to become a profitable business, the private sector will not invest sufficiently in this sector.

Before land reform, agriculture in Iran was the net exporter and was one of the important origins of the exchange earning source for the country, but unfortunately, in recent years, it has become the net importer, for example. In the year 1962, the balance of export and import of agriculture had 979 million rials in surplus but in 1972, it became about 8535 million rials in arrears. It is certain that in later years, this gap widened. In recent years, half of rice and one third of barley and cattle food, sugar and 70% of vegetable oil of domestic needs are imported from foreign countrics.

Private industries are only assembly plants and dependent on oil

As explained in previous chapters, in the last 15 years, a considerable number of basic industries as iron mill and machine tool factories, and also petrochemical complexes had been created by the government in the country. In 1957, the country was producing 600,000 tons of iron and 10 million tons of cement. At the end of the fifth plan, it was decided that iron be produced to attain five million tons, and 20m. tons of cement. The average growth rate of the industrial sector was in those years about 16%. The main part of industries established by the private sector, transport vehicles, home appliances and electronic industries were only assembly plants whose added value was very small and required large amounts of semi-finished products and raw material to be imported from foreign countries and financed by the oil industry. These industries were not independent from a technological point of view, but dependent on foreign sources. Establishment of assembly industries with a small added value caused import of consumer goods to be increased. For example, the imports of consumer goods which was only 400 million dollars in 1962, increased to 12 billion dollars in 1979. This unfavorable change in imports of consumer goods would create for the country great difficulties in the long run when the oil export is declined.

As a result of the extra protection of government, and granting monopoly rights to private industries, there was established in the country many unhealthy industries whose prices of products were high, quality poor and are only dependent on the government's protection and the oil income. In recent years, the assembly industries by concluding clearing agreements of government with socialist countries, have been able to export only the equivalent of 1/30 of their import requirements. The industries of Iran, because of inefficient management and lack of skilled workers, are not able to compete with other countries in international markets and usually their prices are 30% higher and the quality poorer in comparison with similar goods. The ambitious goals of industrial development of the fifth plan without considering possibilities of the country from the view point of skilled human force, electric power, transport facilities, and capacity of ports cuased a considerable part of the country's resources to be wasted and most projects to remain unfinished. For example, in 1975, the cargo ships had to wait more than 100 days beforc to be unloaded and the imported goods after unloading, remained in the rain, and sun and were wasted, because of insufficient warehouses. In this year, over 1.5 billion dollars was paid to ship owners as surcharge for delay in unloading, shortage of transport facility and electric power was an important bottleneck that caused the industries of the country not to be able to operated to full capacity.

The iron mill in Isphahan, purchased from Russia, because it was a very old model, was not economic and every year attains great loss. The petrochemical industry notwithstanding its enormous investment, had not been capable of achieving its development goals. It is estimated that in future plans, communication be considered as first priority, requiring at least 15 years for this sector to match other sectors of the economy of the country.

Because of the vastness of the country, and separation of towns and agricultural areas with long distances, an enormous amount of investments in communications is required and usually ¼ of the public expenses is appropriated for this purpose.

In 1975, the capacity of Irans ports was about 5 million tons and there was 50 thousand miles of roads in the country, only half of them asphalted, and it is estimated that at least 250 thousand miles more asphalted roads are necessary to be constructed. None of Iran's railroads are run with electric power and all of them have only one line. In the fifth plan, it was considered that one road be constructed with 6 lanes from Bandarshahpour to Tehran to the north province and another road as a belt around Tehran.

Telephonic communication between the provinces and also with foreign countries developed greatly and therefore, we can conclude, as far as communication is concerned, the most important bottleneck for economic development is the shortage of good roads and railways.

Education system

As we know, having a good and suitable educational system is high priority for industrial progress. In Iran, in the last 20 years, the number of universities and colleges increased greatly and the number of students during this period has increased more than ten times. Undoubtedly, the quantity was taken into consideration and not the quality. In recent years, constant strikes and manifestations of students prevented them from studying and acquiring the necessary knowledge. There is a shortage of instructors and classrooms, and there are 70 students in each class and an average of 60 students for every teacher.

In the fields of science which is necessary for the development of the country in medicine, engineering, and agriculture, there are more shortcomings, and the knowledge acquired by the students is not suitable with the requirements of economic development and the standard of education is low. In the last twenty years, more than 300,000 students have studied in foreign countries and only 20,000 of them (less than 10%) have returned to the country. In the year before the revolution, about 120,000 Iranian students were studying abroad.

Because of the shortage of instructors and schools, universal education has not progressed as it was expected and about 50% of the people are still illiterate.

Another bottleneck that has hindered economic development, is the shortage of skilled human power due to insufficiency of professional schools in the country. In 1968, more than 100,000 foreign skilled workers were working in Iran and still there was a need for another one hundred thousand of them.

Inequality of incomes among different classes

All groups of people in Iran have not been able to benefit from the fruits of economic growth, and only a minority of people have become very rich. It is estimated that in the early years of the 1970's, 10% of the people have appropriated 40% of the national income for themselves, and in later years that the oil income increased the gap between the rich and the poor widened in Iran.

In most industrial countries, the government publishes two tables to illustrate economic progress. one showing growth of different sectors of the economy and the other showing changes in distribution of income among different groups of people. Because absolute growth of the national income without considering it's impact on the welfare of the people is not desirable and if it causes distribution to be more unequal, it creates more discontent among the people. In Iran, the Central Bank publishes the first table that illustrates only absolute growth of the national income in different sectors of the economy without giving any information about it's distribution.

Inflation and its effects

During the third and fourth plan (1962-1972), the increase of volume of money and current and development expenditures was moderate and although the economy of the country had an average yearly 10% growth rate, prices rose only 2% per year, but in the last two years of the fourth plan, the prices increased 10%. But in 1952, and later on, as a result of an enormous increase in the oil income and injecting it into the economy of the country, volumes of money and credits increased largely and the budget of the government tripled in two years. Although the investment sum considered for the fifth plan at first was more than the volume of investment of the four previous plans, altogether, it was revised and increased to twice the original plan. Such an ambitious plan was out of the country's physical and human resource capacity. Consequently existing inflation, was intensified and rose to 30% per year.

In 1975, in Tehran, rent increased more than 200% and food prices rose about 30%. As a consequence of intense inflation, inequality of incomes became greater and the rich became richer. The rich people spent most of their incomes buying luxury foreign goods and building palaces and buying houses and apartments in foreign countries. In 1976, about 20,000 Iranians bought apartments or houses in London. Contrary to rich people, the ordinary government employees and workers' income shrunk by inflation and they were forced to pay more than 70% of their income for rent of apartments.

During this period, galloping inflation transferred the real purchasing power from those who had fixed incomes or the people whose income was increasing less than the rate of inflation, to those whose income were increasing more than the rate of inflation, therefore, distribution of incomes became more unjust. Furthermore, inflation made distribution of wealth more unequal because the wealth of those people that possessed immovables, gold and tangible assets increased, and on the contrary, the value of wealth of those possessing savings or cash decreased.

Inflation also was detrimental to productive activities, because it encouraged the people to invest in land and other short term speculative businesses. Some people without doing any useful work for the society only by buying and selling land especially in Tehran, acquired great wealth, and having no confidence in the country's future economy, transferred great sums of money to foreign countries.

The public morale deteriorated by inflation and unjust distribution of incomes, so that corruption was widespread among the government employees and materialism became predominant and money replaced moral principles everywhere in the country.

Everyone in the country was trying to conform to the regime, flattering and praising the Shah, in order to obtain the maximum amount of material benefits. The government instead of having an ideology, tried to attract groups of people by providing them material possessions.

The relatives of the king, his court, high officials of government, members of senate, and parliment usually participated in governmental contracts, and so corruption became wide spread in the country. This was undoubtedly one of the main factors of the peoples discontent, that ended at last in the recent revolution.

Foreign trade policy

In formulating the foreign trade policy, the government having at it's disposal vast amounts of oil income, pursued the free trade policy, and as a result of it, every year, the imports increased much more than exports. In recent years, the exports of the country that comprised mostly of raw materials was only five percent of imports and about 95% of imports was financed by exchange earnings of the oil exports.

About 1/3 of the imports consisted of capital goods and 2/3 consumer goods or semi-finished goods and raw materials needed by industries. In the future when the oil exports declines, it is not certain how the government will be able to find enough exchanges to pay for imports.

As discussed in previous chapters, the assembly industries,in order to operate, require every year more than 7 billion dollars raw material and semi-finished products, while they earn only about 2% of it (100 million dollars) by export of a part of their products, therefore, it is certain that these industries are completely dependent on the oil income, in the long run, when the oil reserves of the country are exhausted, they would be faced with great difficulties.

The government of Iran in the last ten years, in formulating the foreign trade policy, was faced with two conflicting policies, to protect domestic industries and agriculture, government was forced to pursue the protection policy, but at the same time to combat inflation and provide sufficient supply of food and essential consumer goods for people, it had to choose the free trade policy; and as a result of this dilemma, the government's foreign trade policy was not consistent and changed continously. The oil income created favorable possibilities for economic growth, but simultaneously, it created some limitations to economic development as inflation, establishment of unhealthy industries, corruption and unproductive but profitable activities.

Financial and fiscal policy of government

Financial policy means, all kinds of activities of government in the fields of economics, welfare, fiscal and development and current budget policies. Today in all countries, the financial policy is the most important tool by which the government can establish equilibrium between general demand and supply of goods and services, government investment and private investment in different sectors of the economy, and by these means, to stabilize prices.

Because the government has at it's disposal vast amounts of oil income in Iran, it's financial policy is more extensive in comparison with most other countries. After the increase of the oil income in 1974, the government budget was about 80% of the national income of the country. During the years of carrying out the fourth plan, the government's budget increased an average of 22% per year. But in the year 1952, the current budget of government increased 47%, investment 24%, and together there was a 39% increase. In 1953, as a result of an extraordinary increase in the prices of oil, the government's income from oil increased four times and at the same time, the budget of the government also tripled in one year.

The government expenditures in rials was financed by the oil income. It was injected from outside into the economy of the country, therefore, it had much expansion effect. Certainly, some part of it was neutralized by imports, but the remainder through increased volume of money and credits created intense inflation. On the whole, the budget of the government (current and development). after the increasing of the oil income, became more than 80% dependent on the oil income.

After increase of the oil income, the government believed that because of having at it's disposal enormous amounts of financial resources, money can solve all problems of rapid development ; therefore, it revised the fifth plan and added to the volume of all projects, and all governmental institutions and ministries expenses' began to increase immensely without taking into consideration the capacity of the physical and human resources of the country. As a result, healthy and steady development was no longer possible, already existing economic establishments faced great perplexities and the result was inflation.

corruption, and waste of resources of the country.

The fiscal policy of the government was not beneficial to the majority of the people, because it was based mostly on indirect taxes that was imposed on all people on essential goods equally, but the companies who had large profits by preparing incorrect accounts, usually showed losses and evaded paying taxes.

Dependence of Iranian economy on foreign countries

Most industries created by the private sector were only assembly plants and therefore, in providing for their operation raw materials, semi-finished products, technology and management are dependent on western capitalist countries, hence, advancement of industrialization in Iran, instead of making the country more self sufficient, it made it more dependent on foreign capitalist countries, and economic dependence was followed by political and cultural dependence.

In Iran, the rich and well-to-do classes usually imitated in consumption the western countries, especially the United States, and they consumed goods similar to those countries, that are imported from abroad that is paid by the oil income or produced by assembly industries. The assembly industries are usually the branches of foreign companies or installed with Iranian and foreign participation, but mostly, technology and production policies and management are in the hands of foreigners that have no interest to transfer management and technology to Iran, in order to benefit from monopoly profits for longer periods. As the interest of Iranian shareholders of assembly industries conincides with the interests of foreign shareholders, there is no incentive to transform assembly plants to independent national industries.

There is technological and managerial dependence on third world countries like Iran to advanced capitalist countries. Doctors in medicine and engineers that have been trained by great expenses from these countries go to western countries, especially the United States and Canada, in order to have better material benefits and a more favorable atmosphere to work. For example, in the last 20 years, more than 300,000 students have been trained in Iran or in foreign countries with Iran's expenses and 80% of them left the country and never returned. Economic dependence is also detrimental to the national culture and traditions because foreign

foreign and internal capitalists through advertisement, publicity and by way of newpapers, films, radio and television, encourage the people to imitate foreigners in consumption and in all aspects of their way of life. From a political point of view, the ruling class and government of these countries are also dependent on foreign countries to provide them arms and other military and political support in order to protect the interests of foreign and internal capitalists.

One of the factors that is effective in creating dependence on third world countries like Iran on capitalist industrial countries are multinational corporations, most of them American. The multinational companies have created some kind of international division of labor on the basis of classes of countries in the world. High jobs and decision making officials are concentrated in some important cities of advanced industrial countries like New York, or London, and they establish in third world countries like Iran branches or other kinds of firms with participation of foreign and internal capital, and decision about what to produce and how much and what price is dictated from the centers. Dependence between the centers of multinational companies and most countries is in the form of one commander and the other obedient and superior and inferior. On the whole, technology, management, and important administrative decisions are in the hands of these centers and these companies in different ways weaken sovereignty, and financial and the monetary policies of host countries where there branches are located, and bring culture and regulations, and laws of these countries under the influence of industrial countries where the main centers of these companies are located; and as a result of it, structure and texture of the third world countries societies are torn, and self sufficiency gives it's place to dependency. The branches of these multipurpose and multinational companies in third world countries like Iran, produce goods mainly for the minority of the rich people, and because their technology is capital intensive, they create employemnt for a small number of people, and also create a dualism economy, and by increasing inequality of incomes, spread discontent among the people.

Increase of inequality of incomes

In Iran, previous to the economic development, the factors of production, i.e., capital, land, technology, natural resources, was owned by a minority of people and simultaneous with economic development, there has been no program to distribute more justly, the wealth and incomes, therefore, the main part of the benefits of economic development was appropriated by a minority of rich people, that created demand for luxury goods and services, either to be imported from foreign countries or produced in the country. Producing luxury goods in the country required skilled intensive and capital intensive technology. Therefore, demand for capital and skilled workers increased, while demand for unskilled workers diminished. Consequently, the income of owners of capital and skilled workers and personnel rose much more than the incomes of unskilled workers, peasants, and governments ordinary employees, hence, the gap between the incomes of those groups and also town dwellers and peasants widened.

Some people believe that unequal distribution of income is favorable to savings and investments, because they think that rich people will save and invest their extra incomes, but this opinion in a country like Iran,that rich people spend most of their incomes in buying luxury goods is not correct. In Iran, private capitalists use considerable amounts of money in unproductive activities like buying and selling land, speculation, and so the resources of the country is not used efficiently to the advantage of all people of the country. The government is also extravagant in luxury consumption. Government investments is spent mostly for the benefit of privileged people living in towns. For example, education and infrastructure expenditures for providing electricity, water, hotels, hospitals, roads, and etc., are spent in big cities and only the residents of those cities benefit from them.

We can conclude, that the resources of Iran in the past instead of being used to provide welfare and a satisfactory standard of living for all groups, is used mostly to satisfy desires of the few privileged minority groups. As a result of this, expectations of people from the increasing of the oil income and economic development is not fulfilled and this has created discontent and conflict between groups and was one of the main factors in creating revolution.

The economic dualism

The economic development in Iran has been mostly concentrated only in some big cities like Tehran, Shiraz, Isphahan, Tabriz and Abadan, and provinces far way from centers like Kerman, Baloutchistan, and also the countryside, has not benefited from economic development and modernization. Therefore, there is dualism of economy in Iran, meaning that there are two kinds of economic activity in Iran side by side, one modern in some big cities and the other traditional, in agricultural areas and small towns. There is in Iran, two separate societies with different cultures and habits. Minority rich people living in cities imitate consumption and the way of life of western countries, and the majority of people have the traditional way of life. People of these two societies do not comprehend each other, and even harbor animosities towards each other.

One of the consequence of economic dualism, is the vast emigration of peasants and small town residents to big cities, especially to Tehran. Two separate communities in Iran ruin and poison each other, for economic development and modernization of cities, tear in pieces and ruin the economic structure of traditional society and in turn the latter by emigrating to the cities takes revenge and creates many problems for administrating the cities.

CHAPTER 13

THE REVOLUTION OF 1978 AND ITS EFFECTS

The year 1978 is a turning point in the destiny of Iran,because in this year, a revolution like a dreadful earthquake trembled the nationality and the very existence of this country.

Iran at this time, was a country of contrasts: on one hand, the country in a short period had made great progress in economic, social, and military fields, and so held an important position among third world countries, and the government intended to carry on some ambitious and immediate projects in order to make Iran one of the advanced industrial countries of the world.

In addition to the economic achievements, Iran

possessing a great arm force, provided herself with prestige and a high position among the neighboring and other countries.

On the other hand, rapid economic progress had created in this country many kinds of unfavorable side effects as: disequilibrium in different economic sectors and social groups, dependence on foreign countries, corruption, inequalities in wealth and incomes, and dualism in economy, and society, that we have discussed in previous chapters.

In recent years, there was a climate of discontent among the majority of people in Iran. Suppression of all kinds of freedoms, by the Shah's government, corruption, injustice, disruption of social traditional values and moral concepts made discontent so wide spread, that when there was a safety valve opened by the observance of human rights, with the insistence of President Carter, it was considered by people as a weakness of the Shah, and so the accumulated discontents manifested in 1978, as a universal explosion and uprising that later was called the "Islamic Revolution". Some people believe that the uprising of the people of Iran in 1978, in which all groups consisting of, employees, students, merchants, religious people, workers with different interests took part, was only a manifestation of opposition to the ruling class especially the Shah, and in a real and meaningful sense, it must not be called a revolution because this uprising had neither a program for the future nor qualified any coherent group to replace the existing regime.

Opinions about the causes of revolution are different and sometimes in contrast with each other. We can divide the causes into two classes: internal and external, discussed briefly as follows:

External causes of revolution

There are many assumptions regarding the external causes of revolution. The most important ones are as follows:

1- One of the most well known opinion is the Green Belt theory. According to this theory, Mohammad Reza Shah, in recent years had become too powerful, independent, and no longer trusted by western powers. Therefore, western powers, in order to prevent an extension of Russian power to the Persian Gulf countries, and keep the Islamic countries in the state of backwardness, in continued efforts to exploit them, planned to substitute the Shah's government with an Islamic anti-communism government.

2- Some other people believed that after the coup of August 1952, United States influence replaced British influence, therefore, the British government in order to acquire influence again in Iran, by way of B.B.C. broadcasting and through the help of some Mullahs, and their traditional friends, made vast propaganda against the Shah and weakened him. They last succeeded to attract the cooperation of the United States and other western countries, so that in the meeting held in Guadolomp, all western powers agreed to overthrow the Shah, and they sent General Heuzer to Tehran to arrange transfer of the government.

3- Some have the opinion that because the oil companies intended to increase the price of oil, they decided to stop Iranian oil production, therefore, they made plots to create insecurity in Iran and weaken the government.

Iranians usually attributed all events to foreigners, because they were suspicious of foreign powers and this is the result of the history of the country, especially in the last two centuries, that all important events in the country occurred through intervention of foreign powers. Most people of Iran have the opinion that difficulties and backwardness of the country, until the Russian revolution was due to the intervention of Tsarist Russian and Britain. After that period, until Mossadegh's government, the influence of Britain prevailed and then followed the present time intervention of the United States government.

At the present, Iranians in Iran or outside Iran called their opponents spies or servants of the United States. This spirit caused Iranians not to be able in all events to face reality and solve their problems. It is certain that the people of this country believe that their fortunes and destiny lie in the hands of others. They have no confidence in themselves and in their ability to solve their problems and improve their situations.

As we have discussed in previous chapters, the main factor that caused a universal uprising in Iran, was the discontent of the people of the years that, at last, ended in revolution. Therefore, we can conclude that the primary elements of revolution, in our opinion, are internal; and external factors were secondary. As long as there was stability in the country, foreign countries, west and east, were supporting the Shah, but when they knew that as a result of universal discontent, stability vanished and the majority of the people no longer supported the king. They began to consider some other alternative to the Shah's regime in order to protect their own interests.

The internal causes of revolution

1- After 1962, the Shah proclaimed some social reform that was approved by the people through referendum, and was implemented by government. Gradually, the power of state was concentrated completely in the hands of the Shah. By carrying out four economic plans, the country achieved great successes in economic and social fields. For example, in less than ten years, the number of industrial units of the country increased from 25,000 to 280,000 and many iron mill, machine tools and petrochemical factories were built. Most towns were provided with healthy water, electric power and other modern facilities; and per capita income of the people increased from 200 dollars to more than 2000 dollars. More or less, all groups benefited from a better standard of living so that the children of workers who previously had no access to any kind of education were studying in universities and colleges in Iran or in foreign countries and the number of students increased enormously and literacy increased from 5% to 40%.

Notwithstanding the above mentioned accomplishments, mainly because of rapid development, some unbalances, shortages, and bottlenecks manifested in the early years of the 1970's. At this time, it was advisable and necessary that the government, instead of continuing the efforts to increase rapid and absolute growth,does its best to remove restraints and shortages in the economy of the country. But in 1973, as a result of the enormous increase of the oil income, the government instead of reducing the growth rate, in order to remove shortages and bottlenecks, suddenly doubled the volume of the fifth plan and intended to carry out the ambitious plans that was out of the physical and human resource capacity of the country. The Shah at this time, was so ambitious that he wanted to transform Iran in a short period from a developing country to one of the most advanced industrial countries second to Japan or Asia. He believed that with a vast amount of financial resources at his disposal, he could do anything and solve any problems. By injecting excessive money to the economy by the existing government, inflation was greatly intensified and as a result of it, the rich became richer and the poor became poorer, and corruption increased. A minority of people acquired enormous amounts of windfall riches and thereby, provided for themselves luxury and splendid living. In addition to the palaces that these people built for themselves, in the northern part of Tehran, they bought houses and flats in some European countries and the United States of America and every year they traveled many times to foreign countries for vacationing and buying luxury goods.

In contrast to the above mentioned minority class, the majority of people, as government employees and retired persons and other low income groups, were not only able to benefit from the oil income, but because their income did not increase as much as the inflation rate, they lost some of their real income.

Furthermore, after the year 1975, due to the economic recession in the world, Iran's export of oil decreased, some projects were stopped, and the economy experienced a slump and inflation at the same time.

In summary, we can conclude, that absolutism, widespread censorship by Savak, corruption, inequality of incomes, discrimination, dependence on foreign countries, and economic and social dualism were the factors that created such universal discontent that ended in revolution.

2- Enmity and suspicion of religious elements against the Pahlavi regime was another factor in the uprising of the people. The efforts of Pahlavi's regime in the last 50 years to modernize Iran and create a secular government had reduced the influence of religion in society, and as a result of it, the power of the religious leaders weakened. Recent rapid economic and social changes of the country increased opposition of them. In fact, the fundamentalists at this time not only wanted to overthrow the Shah, but also to abolished completely the western style of government. For example, the Ayatoullah Khomeini, the leader of the revolution, arriving in Tehran in his first speech in Behishte-Zahra cemetery declared:

> "Pahlavi dynasty has ruined Iran and has only developed the cemeteries; long time and great efforts are necessary to bring the country back to what it was 50 years ago."

But as we know, before Pahlavi's regime, the country had no roads, no railways, no industries, no schools, and universities, no security and no central government. In addition, once in a while, because of lack of any sanitary and health services and healty drinking water, some epidemic diseases as colora, malaria, etc., spread all over the country and killed hundred thousands of people. Also in some years, famine occurred all over the country and a considerable number of people starved to death. In the last famine that appeared before Pahlavi's regime, the people were dying in Azarbaydjan and Tehran from hunger, while in Khosistan provice, the grain harvest was so abundant that the people were forced to burn some of it, because there were no roads, it was not possible to transport it to famine stricken provinces. During Pahlavi's regime, roads, railways and a good communication system all over the country were built, and healthy drinking water for most of the towns was provided and health services developed, therefore, in the last fifty years, no more famine or epidemic diseases appeared in the country. Furthermore, before Pahlavi's regime, 95% of the people were illiterate, there were no universities and women were deprived of most of their social rights, as the right of election. Divorce rights were only in the hands of the men and polygamy was wide spread in the country. Consequently, there is no doubt that in the opinion of religious fundamentalist, all achievements mentioned above was the ruin of the country and therefore, it must go back to fifty years ago.

3- Another cause of the revolution, was aversion and hatred of the majority of the people to the way of life of the upper stratum of society that was linked with luxury, corruption and western style consumption. Because it was foreign to the country, and had divided the country into two separate societies each with a different culture and traditions. The majority of the people who lived traditionally, participated in the uprising against the minority of people living in modern society.

4- Another factor was President Carter's human rights program. He put pressure on the Shah to reduce oppression and observe human rights in the trials of political prisoners, and establish democracy gradually in Iran. The Shah who was dependent on the United States and needed the support of Carter, tried to conform his policy with Carter's views, and reduced his pressure upon his opponents. But the opposition groups regard it as a sign of the Shah's weakness and increased their opposition through open manifestations and strikes.

5- Another cause of revolution was intense opposition of militant religious fundamentalists. Their activities against the regime was disguised before, but when manifested in 1978, it openly succeeded to attract most of the young religious students to their ranks.

Religion in Iran has always been a powerful element in society, and in addition to terrorist activity, as the killing of two prime ministers (Razmara and Mansour), their activities took the form of open manifestation against the government. In the recent uprising of the people, they also organized universal manifestations of millions of people covering the streets of Tehran and other cities by exploiting religious sentiments of illiterate people. The programs of manifestations was well organized. Uprising first began in Tabriz and then by holding the ceremony of the 40th day of memory of those killed in previous manifestations. The manifestations continued to spread to other cities. In 1978, the revolution began with the invasion of governmental buildings, cinemas, banks and liquor shops. The goal of revolution was the negation of everything that belonged to western civilization and also opposition to the upper stratum of society. The organizers of the revolution, by spreading false rumors and using radio broadcasts of other countries especially the British Broadcasting Corporation (B.B.C.) encouraged martyrdom among young people by publishing exaggerated amounts of money that had been sent to foreign countries by the ruling class which weakened the morality of that class.

The methods used for overthrowing the government was so organized, that it was never known in Iran and therefore some people conclude that there were disguised foreign hands at the back of the uprising and revolution.

The goals of uprising of the people

The majority of people as students, government employees, merchants and workers who participated in the manifestations in the year 1978, had no intention to revive the Shiet religion in Iran, but their main aim was to condemn what was foreign in the community and to oppose injustice, exploitation of foreign and internal capitalists, absolutism and discrimination. They also wished to establish freedom, equality, social and economic justic and democracy. Therefore, at the time of the revolution, it was anticipated that after the revolution the liberal elements of the society,deprived from freedom for such long time,would take charge of Iran. At the beginning of the revolution, the religious leader, the Ayatoullah Khomeini, who was residing in Paris, declared his opinion in favor of democratic freedoms as freedom of speech, press, parties and abolition of the secret police (savak). Other organizers of uprisings were presenting the programs that comprised of: establishment of national independent and self-sufficient economy, and strengthening agriculture and real industries. Furthermore, they promised that after the success of the revolution, they would transfer the power of government to civil authorities and as usual, devote their time to religious and moral teachings.

But before long, the Mullahs forgot their promises and by unfounded accusations, eliminated all liberals and specialists from the government and took into their own hands exclusively all organs of governments including lawmaking, executive, judicial and army power. They have put at the head of each government institution one Mullah without having any knowledge about the related institution. The religious fundamentalists who seized the power after the revolution, abolished all kinds of freedoms and closed all kinds of independent newspapers, fired professors and closed universities, and created a formidable police system called Savama to replace Savak. The fundamentalists also created a monopoly party like the old Rastakhiz in the name of the Islamic republican party that intervenes much more than the Rastakhiz party in all aspects of the life of the people.

Also in the new regime, the courts are completely in the hands of Mullahs and without any ceremony, they condemn the people that they consider are opposed to the Islamic regime, without giving them the right to defend themselves. They are put to death, executed instantly and their properties confiscated. Usually, the political opponents are accused of chimeric and unfounded accusations as corrupt of the earth, enemy of god, or spy of foreigns, that according to Mullahs' interpretation of Islam, the only punishment for these kind of guilts is execution and confiscation of property.

The international institutions such as, Human Rights Society or Amnesty International, that previously criticized the Shah's regime, were admired by Mullahs, but today, because they protested the Mullah's inhuman treatment with their opponents, they are accused of being the servants of Imperialism.

Again, in the last three years, the prisons in Iran are filled with political prisoners, and now torture, confiscation of property and executions of opposition is so wide spread in Iran that it never had any precedence in the country's history. Most of the intellectuals, knowlegeable men as professors, doctors in medicine, engineers and others, having no security in Iran left the country, and at the present, more than one million of them are living in western countries.

Actions of the Islamic republic in Iran and it's political, social, and cultural effects.

1- Enmity with nationalism and Iranian culture:
The Mullahs who have taken the power of government in Iran condemned nationalism, and they despise nationalists and liberals. The new regime has changed the names of all streets, universities, hospitals and ports from the old Iranian great men as Ferdoci, Hafiz, and Saadi to Arabian names as Yaserarafat, and Abouzar. The Pahlavi street in Tehran, at the beginning of the revolution was named Mossadegh Avenue. After a short time, it was changed again, to a religious name of Valieh Assr (the name of shiet twelve Imam).

From the Iranian culture which was related to the pre Islamic period, was procalimed by Mullahs as blaspheme and heresy, but also great master pieces of Irans history, philosophy and literature created by well-known men as Ferdossi, Molavi, Khayam and Hafiz, that was the pride of Iran which threatened the new regime with insolence and total suppresion. In the schools, the teachers are instructed to erase the names of Kourosh and Anoushiravan, the great Kings of Iran from the books, and also to replace the name of Takhat Jamshid with the name of "Ruins near Shiraz". The Iranian national flag of white, red and green with the lion and sun on it which had no relationship with the old regime, is a symbol of nationalism of Iran has also changed. Furthermore, all kinds of arts, such as music, painting, dance and everything that makes people happy are condemned, as being "opium of brain", and therefore, are eliminated from the radio and television of Iran.

Some believe that the damages incurred to the Iranian culture by Mullahs is the most destructive action of the revolution, and they argue that economic and material damages are reparable in the long run, but the destruction of a nation's culture is disruptive to its very existence.

Nationalism in Iran, is the only means of unification of all the people of Iran, that are of different ethnic, religions, culture and languages, and in contrast to the opinion of the present regime, the

Shiet sect of Islam could not replace it, because a considerable number of Sunnits secot of Islam, and also followers of other religions as Christians, Jews, Zorastrians and Bhaeis, live in Iran, all are Iranians, and until this revolution, they were living in peace side by side. We believe that loving the country is not in contrast with Islam, and the real Islam inspires love, freedom and moral virtues, but what in the name of Islam is presented today as Islam in Iran, consists of violence dogmatism, revenge, enmity to science and modernism. Therefore, to be a true Musliman it is not necessary to be against nationalism, history, and the culture of the country. For example, although the city of Romeis, the capital of the catholic sect of christian religion, the people living in that city respect greatly the historical monuments of ancient Rome, and do their best to protect them. The communist countries also protect their past cultural and historical riches with great attachment.

2- Reestablishment of censor and abolishment of all kinds of freedom- One of the principle causes of discontent among the people that ended in universal uprising, was the existence of widespread censoring, exaggerated propaganda of government, and monopolizing of political activity to Rastakhiz party in the old regime. Therefore, the people of Iran expected that after the revolution all kinds of censoring would be abolished and all parties, and associations could enjoy freedom. But the new regime like the old one, closed all parties and newspapers not belonging to itself, and organized a monopoly party named "Islamic republican party" and also taking in its own hands radio and television, and began to broadcast false propaganda and extended it's control to all aspects of life of the people to such an extent, that the old regime with all it's shortcomings was acquitted. During the last three years in Iran, the spirit of brotherhood and affection is substituted with enmity, hate, revenge. The parents are asked by Mullahs to spy on their children and their neighbors.

3- Invasion on universities and closing all of them

The new regime, has closed nearly all colleges and universities, and has treated the professors, specialists, and researchers with insolence, and in the name of cleaning, had dismissed most of them, nearly half of them have left the country; and as a result of it, the country is affected by scientific, cultural and technical shortage and poverty. Also tuition and scholarship of most of the students studying in different fields of science in foreign countries was cut and they were forced to work as waiters in restaurants or hotels and shops instead of finishing their education.

4- Cleaning government institutions and education systems: In the name of "cleaning", government has laid off hundred thousands of experienced and specialized personnel in administration of universities and schools, and this policy led to the emigration of many thousands of doctors in medicine and in other fields of science and engineers to European and American countries, and as the prime minister of Canada has declared in his interview with journalists, this action of Iranian government has been a great valuable present from Iran's revolution to some industrialized western countries, that it's real worth is more than many billions of dollars.

5- Revolutionary courts: The procedure of these courts is to condemn the political dissidents without a true trial and giving the accused the right to choose an attorney and defend himself, from death and confiscation of their properties. Usually, the condemnation to death is based on unfounded, chimeric and ambiguous accusations as corrupt on the earth and enemy of God. Torture of political prisoners according to Amnesty International is very common in the prisons. Even according to the evidences gathered by international organizations as, Human Rights society and Amnesty International, even the boys and girls of 12 years old are accused of participation in manifestations or distributing prints against government or sympathizing with illegal parties, have been put to death without even asking their identities. According to the report of the Amnesty International Society, until this date, more than 5000 have been executed and the properties of more than 400,000 people have been confiscated in Iran by the order of the revolutionary courts. Certainly the real number of executions has been much more than what is declared officially, as the leader of Midjahidin declared in Paris, most of the executions are not declared by the government, and according to his findings, the number of executions is about 13,000 in the last three years. Some prisoners are so severly tortured that they are killed, and after being dead they are executed in order to hide the torture and their bodies are not delivered to their families. Therefore, executions, torture and treatment of prisoners with insolence and inhuman methods is so widespread in this regime that the old regime with all its shortcomings is considered as democratic and a freedom loving regime.

6- Depriving women of their rights: The women, half of the population of Iran, in the past centuries suffered greatly and their human and social rights have been denied in those periods. During the Pahlavi regime, their position had improved especially by approval of the family protection law and it's implementation. Polygamy has been restricted, divorce was no more, only in the hands of the man and woman participated in constructive economic and social life, side by side. But the new regime has abolished the family protection law and again polygamy and temporary marriage is legalized and the women are deprived of having access to most jobs.

7- Ill treatment of minorities: The ethnic and religious minorities, in the past had been living in peace with other Iranians, now it is violated by the new regime and a considerable number of them have been imprisoned, tortured, and even executed for pursuing this inhuman policy the Mullahs have damaged the reputation of Islam in the world.

The ethnic minorities as Kurds, Turkamans, Beloutchy, are demanding self-rule and autonomy in their internal affairs. The government instead of discussing with them and solving the problem in the framework of Iran's nationality peacefully, has declared war on them and killed a considerable number of Kurd. This has weakened Kurd's attachment to Iran. The country still continues to face the dangers of separation.

8- Isolation of the country from world community by taking hostages: The Iranian government contrary to international rules and principles, ignored the political immunity of political personnel of the Foreign Embassy, and in order to divert the attention of the people from it's failure to accomplish the goals of revolution, and also to accuse their opponents as foreign elements, has captured the personnel of the American embassy and held them more than one year as hostages. This action had not only resulted in billion of dollars of economic loss, but also caused the isolation of Iran from the international community, and introduced the Iranians as savages and oppressors, on the contrary, the Americans being oppressed and law abiding people. At last after 14 months, according to the agreement in Algeria, the hostages were freed, but Iran from this action sustained economic, financial and moral losses.

9- The economic losses of Iran: During these years of Islamic government, the economy of the country sustained such great disruptions that it is estimated that even with great effor for two generations, it would not be possible to repair the damages. According to available statistics, the most important economic damages are as follows:

A- Industries- The majority of industries of Iran, such as: the steel factory of Ahvaz, the greatest refinery in the Middle east in Abadan, iron industry in Isphahan, petrochemical complexes in Khosistan, machine tool factories and tractor factories, are all badly damaged by war with Iraq, or because of lack in raw materials, mismanagement and shortage of specialists and skilled workers, that left the country. Hundreds of unfinished projects are standing still, and some industries that operate continue their operation with only 30% of their capacity. Consequently, more than 3 million workers are out of work and those who are working, are in reality, disguised unemployed.

It is esitmated that during the last three years, more than 50 billion dollars worth of capital is wasted in Iran. Most operating industries are in a state of bankruptcy. For example, according to the declaration of a Tavakoli minister of labor of Islamic government, the Iran national automobile factory that before the revolution had nearly one billion rials yearly profit at the present, has more than 5 billion rials loss, and this factory is not able to pay the wages of its workers; therefore, the workers have threatened to strike but Mr. Tavakoli had declared," In Islam, there is no place for unions and strikes, and if the workers attempt to strike, the factory would be closed permanently."

B- Intense and galloping inflation: According to statistics published by the Central Bank of Iran, the rate of inflation in the last three years has been around 75% and last year only 25%. But certainly, the official figures are not indicative of real facts, because rationing nearly all consumer products in the country has created an active black market for them, many times at the official prices. Therefore, if we take into consideration the prices of black markets and th rate of inflation in the last three years, it would be more than 300%.

One of the main causes of intense inflation is unlimited printing of banknotes by the government without having the cover. Another factor is the decrease of industrial and agricultural production in the country. In spite of the cancellation of most government expenditures such as: all development projects are cancelled, considerable number of employees are laid off, salaries of most civil or army retired persons are no longer paid, yet the government suffers of a large budget and balance of payment deficit, and as a result of it, the reserves of the country at the beginning of the revolution was about 12.5 billion dollars, at the present, it is less than 1 billion dollars, and the government has been forced recently to sell its gold reserves and historical jewels and treasures of the country. The value of the money of the country has become so worthless internally and externally that in the free markets, the dollar is exchanged for rials at five times it's official value. The above facts show that Iran at the present, from a economic, financial and monetary point of view is in the threshold of bankruptcy, and the regime has not only succeeded to raise the standard of living of the poor people, but has made the rich and middle classes alo poor. The people today spent most of their time in long lines buying bread, meat, vegetables, soap, oil and other essential consumer goods and suffered greatly from inflation and shortages.

C- Decline of agricultural products: Agricultural activity also during the last three years has declined and only in the last year has agricultural production decreased 20% in comparison with previous years, and as a result of it, the food shortage is so intense in the country, that the government has been forced to import some of it's food requirements from such countries as Israel and the United States, in spite of the fact that the government everyday shows enmity against those countries.

D- Unemployment situtation: In the last three years, because of the closing down of most industries, development projects, and dismissing a great number of employees with the pretext of cleaning, unemployment, has increased to unprecedented figures. It is estimated that there are at least 3 million unemployed, We have to add to this figure, 2 million that have fled from war zones and live in camps and 1.5 million emigrants.

E- Imports and exports: In the years after the revolution, because of the decrease of the oil exports and exports of other products, the exchange earning of the country has lowered considerably, but on the contrary, imports of consumer goods have increased greatly. In the year 1977, the country was exporting daily 5 million barrels of oil, and at that time, the value of imports was 16 billion dollars, of which the main part was capital goods and raw materials needed for economic development. But in 1980, the export of oil was only 900,000 barrels per day, and other exports had been reduced about 50%, imports increased 26%, most of it was consumer goods and balance of payment was in great deficit, and the deficit was financed by exchange reserves of the country, and the country has become dependent on consumer goods especially food, more than before the revolution, from foreign countries.

On the whole, the economic situation of the country is in such bad shape that it has created universal discontent and the government until the present time, has been able to prevent manifestations and strike of workers only by terrorism, executions and censorship.

F- Disruption of arm forces and the war with Iraq: Irans defense power before the revolution was so strong that it was considered one of the greatest powers in Asia, and Iran was called Gendarm of the Persian Gulf, and all its neighbors respected it and never dared to trespass Iran's borders. For example, Iraq that had a long time dispute over controlling Shattel ell Arab river, was forced to conclude agreement with Iran, and accept Iran's control to that river. During the revolution, the defense force of Iran was disrupted and greatly damaged. The revolutionary courts with encouragement from leftist groups executed most of the high officers of the army and many pilots, and they sentenced others to long term imprisonment or dismissed them from the army, only for being in the army of the Shah, and so weakened the army of the country. The government of Iraq considering, the situation in Iran is favorable for them, and also seeing that Iran is isolated from the world community, and also to prevent the Iranian government's instigation of Shiet sect in Iraq, which is nearly half of it's population, against Iraq government, and export of Iran's revolution to that country, invaded Iran and the war began between two Islamic and neighboring countries that is continuing still at the present time.

As a result of this war, both countries sustained great damages, more than 100,000 people were killed from both sides, some important towns of Iran like Khorramshahr, Abadan, Ahvaz, and Dezful have been ruined. The great refinery of Abadan and petrochemical complexes and other factories in Khosistan are ruined and it is estimated that total damage of this war only for Iran is about 100 billion dollars. In addition, because some parts of the country are occupied by foreign forces, about two million people fled from their homes, and now are living in the camps in other parts of the country. This war between two Muslim countries only is to the benefit of Israel and the greal colonizing powers of west and east.

To summarize the effects of the revolution, it can be said that the revolution in a short time was diverted by fundamentalist Mullahs from its goals; (that was, to establish democracy, freedom of speech, press and organizing parties, abolishing inequalities and discriminations, and providing for the country an independent and prosperous economy), to monopolize backward looking government of reactionary and funda mentalist Mullahs. These people have ruined the national culture, stopped economic development, and have treated intellectuals and learned men and women with insolence. The reactionary government being against science and modern civilization, closed colleges and universities, and forced the brains of the country to leave Iran and have encouraged the people to spy on one another and established instead of love, tolerance and brotherhood, revenge, intolerance, especially to ethnic and religious minorities, and fanaticism.

Fundamentalists who have taken the power of government, instead of promoting sciences and establishing social justice and laying the foundation of independent, strong and healthy economy, that without these performances, no country could be an independent and prestigious among the worlds nations. They want to govern the country and rule the people by gathering the people in cemeteries like Beheshte-Zahra and weeping, and chanting slogans against imperialism in the streets of Tehran.

There is no doubt that this regime in the long run, because of being in contrast with Iranian culture and needs of human progress, is doomed to failure, as history shows, civilization never repeats itself.

In order to understand why the revolution has gone astray, we have to consider the features of the Iranian character: The Iranian character generally speaking, has two quite different features: One feature is the art loving, creative talent of philosophy and mysticism, moral concepts, tolerance, hospitality and desire to be in touch with other nations and benefit from the culture and civilizations of other countries. But the other feature of the Iranian character is sentimental, irrational, suspicious of foreigners, and worried about life after death and glorifying martyrdom.

Unfortunately, in this revolution, the latter negative feature of the Iranian character is manifested and the Mullahs have been capable of misuing these negative sentiments and religious beliefs of the people especially illiterates that still comprise nearly half of the population, and change the direction of the revolution in order to have the monopoly power of government. But there is no doubt that this situation is temporary and could not last for a long time, because the sentiments of people that are easily stimulated is also easily changeable.

Furthermore, the intellectuals, and middle classes that comprise a considerable part of the population, and in no country without participation of them is possible to rule the country, are discontent and uneasy about the present situation in Iran, and they do not believe the intervention of Mullah in governing the country. Therefore, the hope of the country to be saved from this misfortune is in the hands of the above mentioned classes and also the manifestation of the positive side of the spirit and characters of Iranians.

As we know by the Arabs invasion, the Sassaniy dynasty was overthrown, the palaces ruined and the treasures of Iran plundered by Arabs, but the Arabs had not been able to conquer the spirit of the Iranians. Arabs, Mogol, and others were like guests that governed Iran for a while and later, they went away without taking Iran away with them. Therefore, there is hope again for the invincible feature of the Iranian spirit, comprising of brotherhood, tolerance, love of reason, philosophy, art progress, and culture to manifest itself and force the Mullahs to leave the government to the civilians and do their own business, and establish a just balance between spritual, moral and material affairs in the country.

This prospect would be realized on the condition that the superpowers for their own egotistic purposes, to have access and exploit Iran's oil reserves, do not intervene in internal affairs of Iran, otherwise, this country would be in danger of separation. To prevent Iran of having such an inauspicious future, it is the duty of all groups of people to put aside any kind of differences that they have in ideology, tastes or kinds of government that they prefer, and together, hand in hand, through all their efforts save the country and establish a progressive, democrative government with participation of all groups, and leave the determination of the kind of regime of Iran to the will of the people.

CHAPTER 14

THE BASIC IDEAS FOR CREATING A WELFARE STATE

The main purpose of this book is to present an economic development program for the purpose of providing welfare and a good life for all Iranian people. There is such a close relationship between economic and political and social issues that it is impossible to carry out an economic program in vacuum. It should be implemented in a framework of a suitable political and social regime, therefore, in this chapter, we are going to discuss the principles and the political and social regime that is most desirable for this purpose, continued in the next chapter, and in the next three chapters, we will discuss the economic development program for establishing the welfare state in Iran.

Furthermore, as the most opposition groups, to present government of Iran, have proposed programs for recontruction of Iran usually are using some expressions regarding ideas and principles as: social justice, freedom and democracy, are expressing them in ambigious and in a general manner, and there is danger in the future to be interpreted by different persons in different ways, and also as most people of Iran still are not acquainted with these expressions. Therefore, in this chapter we are going to discuss, six important ideas and principles that are used in most programs and also are inserted in constitutional laws of most democratic countries. In the next chapter we will discuss democracy and its conditons that it is believed to be the most suitable political regime that can provide happiness and a good life for all people.

The ideas that most other ideas and moral values originate

Plato believed that there are two separate worlds: First, the sensitive world of changing physical things that we comprehend by means of our five senses, and the other world of insensible but intelligible objects, that we comprehend by means of our intellects or mind, as idea of truth or freedom.

For him, both are real worlds, and calling them real worlds means that they exist independently of our understanding them. That is why in Plato's view, the idea of goodness or justice has a complete reality. Plato even believed that the world of ideas has a superior grade of reality in comparison with physical things. He argues that the physical things that we perceive through our senses come into being and pass away and they are continually changing in one way or another, so they have no permanence. But the ideas that are objects of thought are not subject to changes. For example, the ideas of justice or liberty, though we may change our minds about them, they are permanent and are the same at all times and all places, but the physical objects like a house or car, even the stars, change and one day disappear. Plato also believed the world of changing physical things are as a mere shadow of the much more real world of ideas.

The ideas are usually of two kinds, some of them are only subjective, that are different with the different individuals as dreams of people when they are sleeping, but some others have objective reality and could be perceived by all people like justice and freedom. Certainly, two individuals that speak about freedom and justice may each speak about different aspects of those ideas.

Neverthless, both of them are speaking about one real object that is justice or freedom. The only mistake of Plato was that he considered that even without thinking an d existence of thought, the ideas would exist, while if there is no human being to think, the world of ideas also would cease to exist.

Mathematics deals with ideal objects, and not real things, as the square root of minus one, and by this method, discovers the truths that are applicable in economic and social sciences and gives us results that are useful in our everyday life. Those branches of the natural and social sciences that apply mathematics, such as mathematical physics and econometrics, are not only among the most exact sciences, but also the most fruitful in production of results.

Philosophy, religion and morality like mathematics, deal with ideal objects that are beyond the reach of sense perception. Neverthless, as in the case of mathematics, this fact does not prevent them from being useful about experience of reality in matters as human behavior and social institutions and knowing the nature. The better our understanding of ideas, especially the great ideas, the better we understand reality because of the light they throw on it, and we would be able by the help of those ideas to administer better our social and private life and make exact judgement about human problems and moral issues.

Some have the opinion that the discussion about philosophical and moral issues is the business of specialists, but as philosophical and moral concepts are applicable in practical life of everyone, and all persons use them every day without knowing the exact meaning of them, therefore, in order for the citizens to be able to perform their duties as thoughtful human beings, it is necessary that they understnad the meaning of them and for this purpose, teaching philosophy and moral ideas in schools is urgent.

In this chapter, we are going to discuss the six great ideas and principles that originate other moral values. The most important six ideas are: truth, goodness, beauty, liberty, equality and justice.

The above ideas are mentioned in the constitution act of democratic countries and it is agreed by people to respect them by the government and all citizens. For example, in the historical declaration of independence of the United States, some of these ideas are mentioned as below: "We the people of the United States of America believe in this Truth that all human beings are created equal and have some inalienable rights as, freedom, right to live and search of happiness (good life). Also in the introduction of the constitution act of the United States, the main duties of government is mentioned as follows: "establishment of justice, liberty, and providing a good life for all."

Understanding the true meaning of the above mentioned ideas and their observance by government and also by members of society is urgent for every society that wishes to provide welfare, happiness and a good life for all citizens.

The six ideas consist of two groups and each group is comprised of three ideas as below:
First group: truth - goodness - beauty
Second group: liberty - equality - justice

The two groups are essentially different from each other, and in each group, one has dominance over the other two. In the first group, the truth has dominance over goodness and beauty, and in the second group, justice has dominance over equality and liberty.

Usually, by the help of the three ideas: freedom, equality and justice, we are able to organize and live our life in the society. The society that succeeds to carry out all these three ideas completely would be an ideal society, but unfortunately, there is great differences between an ideal society and the existing societies at present. Although the human being during history has made efforts to observe these ideas, sometimes, it has been to some extent successful and sometimes it was laced with failure.

Certainly if a person lives like Robinson Crusoe, in an isolated island alone, he would not require, justice, equality, or liberty, but because a human being is a social animal and is living in societies with others on the basis of competition and cooperation, he is in need of these ideas. For this reason, in all democratic societies, special attention is paid to these principles and the respect of these ideas is confirmed in their constitutional law and also in other laws.

The three ideas: truth, goodness, and beauty are the ideas that by the help of them, we make judgment about all other values and ideas, while by other three (justice, equality and liberty) we organize our lives and societies. Even if a person lives alone in an isolated place, he would be in need of the three ideas of truth, goodness and beauty, in order to understand whether there is any truth in the world and to distinguish what is good or bad and what is beautiful or ugly. Thinking about the latter ideas is thinking about the nature and all the world and admiring the beauty of it.

The above discussion shows us that the major difference between the ideas of the first group (truth, goodness and beauty) with the ideas of the second group (justice, equality and liberty) is this: the first ones are used in human relations with all the world and the second is used in human relations with other humans.

With the help of the above mentioned six ideas, we can make judgement about other values and ideas, for example, if we want to distinguish the difference between science, opinion and taste, we have to understand everyone of them and how it relates with the idea of truth. We must have in mind that methods of discovering truth in different problems is different. For example, the method to find the truth in mathematics, and physcis, chemistry is quite different from philosophy, religion and morality. The idea of goodness is useful to perceive some other ideas, such as to distinguish the good person from the bad person, good habits from bad habits. The beauty field is nature, arts, literature and all other things that we envy to hear or contemplate. Below we are going to discuss each of two groups separately:

Group one: Truth - Goodness - Beauty:

Truth

When we are asserting something; it will be considered truth if: first we have no intention of deceiving anybody and also we do not speak against what we think or believe. Second, if there is a perfect relationship with what we are saying and with reality. Some people are so skeptical that they believe, there is no truth in the world and nothing is comprehensible and everything is imagination. The Greek philosopher in ancient times had this opinion, His name was Pyrnha and therefore today this kind of philosophy is called after his name Pyronnian. This opinion is rejected by philosophers and scholars because they believe that today it can not be acceptable. But some philosophers like David Hume have attempted to draw a line between Pyrronism (the extreme skepticism) and moderate form of skepticism that wisdom recommends, because it arises from the fallibility of the human mind, that is incapable of attaining the whole truth.

Also, some people say that something may be true for me and not true for you, or some fact may have been true sometime ago but not now. These propositions are not correct, because they have supposed the truth as a subjective and imaginary object but not reality. This misinterpretaion arised from the failure to distinguish between the truth and falacy which is inherent in a statement and the judgment that a person makes with regard to the truth or the fallacy of the statement in question. We may differ in our judgment about what is true, but that does not affect the truth of the matter itself. For example, a difference of opinion about the number of sheep in a herd may occur, as one person sets the number at fifty, but the others say, not so. In this case, the number of sheep in that herd is a definite number and therefore a truth, but the statement of the person setting it fifty may be true or false. Here the mistake in judgment of one person does not make any difference in the truth and we could discover the truth by enumerating the number of sheep. In another example, it is possible that one jury verdict rules a person guilty and the other rules the person innocent. In reality, the accused person is guilty or innocent and the mistake of a jury does not change the truth. For arriving to discover the truth in this case, it is necessary to try to gather all evidences and witnesses.

In the middle ages, the people believed that the earth was flat, but the earth was spheric, and that erroneous opinion made no change in the spherical shape of the earth. Therefore, we can conclude, that what is changeable is our judgment and opinion and not the reality of truth.

From time to time, an objective truth may change, for example, the population of a country is changeable from time to time, but the statement about the size of a country's population at a given time remains true even when at a later time it has increased in size, if it was accurate in the first place, some times the change is only in our minds and not in reality, but sometimes reality itself changes as when a new species of living organism comes into existence or existent specy as dynassors who became extinct.

The fact that we differ in our judgments and change them from time to time should awaken us to the wisdom of cautious restraint not to regard our judgments as certain and secure and incorrigible. A statement is either true or false objectively, but when subjectively we judge a statement to be true or false, we may do so with more or less assurance, and may speak of it as being more or less true, or we may say that the probability of it's being true is greater or less.

The form of skepticism that wisdon recommends we adopt, is one that does not challenge the objectivity of truth, but it helps us recognize how few are the judgments concerning what is true for which we can rightly claim certitude, and how many fall in the realm of doubt where they are subject to change and correction by all the means that human beings employ in their efforts to get at the truth. In fact, it is only in the realm of doubt that we engage in the pursuit of truth.

In asserting a truth about things and facts, we must always have in mind that it may not be the absolute truth and it is necessary to have a reasonable doubt about it and permanently do our best with the help of thought, reasoning, experience, observance, gathering evidence, information, statistics and analysis everyday to succeed to be nearer to the absolute truth. Furthermore, we have to accept that the opinions of others may be nearer to the truth than ours, therefore we must have tolerance to hear the opinions of others and by exchanging opinions to better discover the truth.

In our daily life, we are obliged to accept the truths as evidence shows us, but at the same time, we must take into consideration that the truth may change by new evidence in the future and in this case, we have to accept the new truth. For example, in regards to health and treatment of diseases, political, economic, and social issues, we should decide on the basis of existent experience, informations and statistics. We frequently act on judgments that are not beyond a reasonable doubt, but are simply more probable than their opposites. In the light of the evidence available at the time and in the light of the best thinking we have done so far, we regard them as more likely to be true. The critical caution we must exercise is contained in the words "at the time" and "so far". These words reminds us that the future always holds the possibility of additional evidence and better thinking , either of which may shift the weight of probability in the opposite direction.

Discovering truth in various disciplines by different methods

In different disciplines or learning the pursuit of truth is accomplished by different methods: For example, the way in which mathematicians arrive at new and better formulations has little in common with the ways in which historians make new findings. Different from both are the procedures of the experimental sciences and the data-gathering routines of the social sciences. The students of all branches of sciences continually make efforts to discover new truths and add them to the body of established truths already achieved or to replace less accurate formulas, or facts with better ones, and by all such steps, singly or together, the sphere of truths agreed upon enlarges and comes closer to be the whole truth, but in no time will the whole truth be attained by human beings.

Viewing the pursuit of truth, we find that, the experts who are competent to judge, as the mathematicians, scientists, historians, each in their own fields of learning have reached agreements about a lot of judgments that they have come to regard as settled or established truths in their respective fields, but usually, they have disagreements in other issues. Those judgments that experts in one field have agreed upon is considered the truth, but those that they have disputed are necessary to investigate, and criticize in order to solve the disputes and achieve the new truths that would be added to the old ones. This does not mean, of course that all these agreed-upon truths have finality. It means that only the shadow of doubt still exists and the future may change the truth.

The sphere of truth, in short, is the sphere of those matters of which we think disagreement is profitable, precisely because we think these matters are possible to resolve differences of opinion and to reach agreement.

There are matters of a different sort, of which we think the very opposite. These are matters of taste rather than matters of truth. There is no point in arguing matters of taste, because our differences of opinion are irreconcileable. Arguing about such matters will not bring us into agreement. On the contrary, we should wisely live with them and tolerate differences of opinions that express divergent tastes. In regards to matters of truth, dispute is fruitful, and we should be prepared to argue with those who disagree with us, with the hope that our disagreement can be solved. We should never abandon our effort to reach the agreement in all matters that fall within the sphere of truth rather than the sphere of taste. To give up is to abandon the pursuit of truth. We should never rest satisfied with anything less than the agreement of all experts about matters belonging to special departments of knowledge. Unanimous agreement is the appropriate condition of the human mind with regard to anything that is a matter of truth rather than a matter of taste.

The matters belonging to mathematics are in the sphere of truth and disagreements should be solved by recourse to rational process, employing the methods and techniques of their disciplines. At the opposite extreme, clearly belonging to the sphere of taste, are such matters as cuisine, social manners, styles in dress, patterns in family life, and so on. Here we do not expect the people to make efforts for solving their differences of tastes. In these matters, uniformity is not desirable. On the contrary, pluralism is the rule of nature. The adoption of one style rather than another is an act of choice, conditioned from cultural, and emotional differences in different societies and individuals.

The sphere of truth is transcultural, transnational, and global. The agreements of those experts who are competent to judge in the fields of mathematics and experimental sciences transcend all national boundaries as well as as ethnic ideological and cultural barriers that separate groups of mankind. In the sphere of taste, mankind is divided into a multitude of factors and is likely to remain in the future.

We have employed mathematics on one hand, and cooking or styles of dress on the other hand, to exemplify,as clearly as possible, the opposite poles at which lie the sphere of truth and the sphere of taste. Between these polar extremes, philosophical opinions and religious beliefs occupy a middle ground.

Some experts regard philosophy and religion as taste, but the philosphers and religious people consider them as truth and claim that the truths of philosophy and religion have nothing to do with special culture or environment. They also argue that like other scientists, they try to resolve their disagreements with rational thinking and arguments.

In religious matters, everybody knows differences of opinion are not solved by discussion or investigation. They are based mostly on emotions, circumstances of society, history, and therefore, nearly 100% of the people have the religion of their parents and consider that they have only the whole truth and other religions are false. It seems that philosophy and religion are composite of half truth and half taste. For example, with regard to religion, that part of it, that consists of moral concepts, as believing in one intelligent creator, or being honest and kind to all human beings and so on, as all experts in different religions agree upon, might be considered in the sphere of truth; but the other part of religion that comprises the laws of regulations and instructions about the material life of human beings as economic, social problems, because they are different in various religions and it is not possible that experts agree upon those differences and because of changes in techniques and circumstances during time, social and economic problems require different solutions, and it is impossible to have eternal laws and regulations for those fields, therefore, that part of religion must be considered as taste or faith, but not the whole truth.

The above discussion shows that in a society comprising of groups of people who have different religions, in order that they may live peacefully with one another, every group must respect the religions of others and also, it is necessary that the majority tolerates minority, ethnic and religious groups.

In democratic societies, the community is composed of different religions, therefore, the sphere of religion is separated from the sphere of politics, economics and social issues, in order to create brotherhood and close ties between the citizens of different religions, to enable the authorities to formulate the laws and regulations on the basis of wisdom, suitable with the requirements of the time and circumstances of the country.

We can conclude, that when somebody asserts an opinion, we must distinguish that the opinion is related to truth or taste and if it was in the sphere of truth, we should by appropriate methods, distinguish that it conforms with truth or not. In the case, we have to accept it otherwise, we have to reject it, but if the opinion is in the sphere of taste or emotions, it is better without discussion to respect it. The principle of tolerating and respecting the religions and tastes of others is one of the essential conditions of a democratic society.

Real good and apparent good

Some philosophers and social scientists, as Thomas Hobbes and Benedict Spinoza, have the view that "good" is merely the name we give to those things that in fact we desire, therefore goodness is not a discoverable property of the things themselves. According to the taste or opinion of different people, something may be considered good or bad. Since desires and aversions are matters of individual temparaments, or nurture, there is nothing that all human beings agree upon as deserving to be called good or bad.

Aristotle,on the contrary, believes that if we desire the right thing, then that thing would be good. Therefore, according to his belief, to distinguish good from bad, first we must distinguish between right desire and unright desire.

Socrates gives us another criterion, there are two kinds of "good" one the real good, and the other apparent good. He reminds us that, our regarding something as "good" because we in fact desire it, does not make it really good. It may, and often does, turn out to be the opposite. What appears to be good at the time we desire it may prove to be bad for us at some later time. Therefore, the fact that we happen to desire something may make it appear good to us at the time, but does not make it really good for us.

The real good is the desire in our human nature, rooted in potentialities and capacities that drive or tend to fulfill. These kinds of desires are presented in all human beings, as engrained properties of human nature, but they always have a tendency towards fulfillment whether we are conscious or not. On the other hand, there are the desires that each individual acquired in the course of his life, as a result of his individual experiences, conditioned by his temperament and by the circumstances of his individual life. Consequently, unlike natural desires which we may not be conscious at a given time, we are always conscious of our acquired desires at the time they are motivating us in one direction or another.

We can use the word "needs" for our natural desires and the word "wants" for the desires we acquire. All human beings have the same specifically human needs, whereas individuals differ from one another with regard to the things they want.

The natural needs are always good because they are real goods. But the acquired wants may be good or bad. For example, acquiring knowledge is always good because it is real good, but smoking a cigaret is an acquired want and is apparent good but really bad.

Most people do not desire the things that they really need, although they are real goods and on the contrary, they want the things that they do not need really and are only apparent good. A human being should not desire as far as possible the things that he does not need, especially when wanting them prevents him from having the things that he really needs. Furthermore, for acquiring the real things, it is necessary to have favorable circumstances, for example, having good health requires favorable and healthy environment and only our desire is not sufficient.

To make the distinction between the real good from apparent good, we have to know the nature of the human being and its relation with environment. We can conclude from the above discussion that even moral concepts are real good, on condition that they conform to the natural needs of the human being, for example, when we say that acquiring knowledge is good, it is real good because it is one of our natural needs.

The "good" might be the things that we need to have or it may be related to our action or behavior, or at last, might be being a good person. Health and acquiring science and having good habits are among the real goods. On the contrary, desiring the unnecessary things as luxury living is only apparent good. The good human is a person that uses all his capabilities to become a good human being and makes efforts to acquire good habits so that he always desires real goods and abstains from having possessions that prevents him of having good things or a good life.

As we said before, having good things is not always possible without the existence of favorable conditions in the society that we are living in, therefore, in the constitution act of most countries is confirmed that providing favorable circumstances for a good life of all members of society is one of the essential duties of the government.

To summarize, we can say, being a good human being, having a good life and having a good society, all are interdependent to one another, because for having a good society, it is necessary that the members of that society have good qualities and living in a good society is essential for a good life.

Good things are sometimes the goal, as having wisdom, or knowledge, and somethimes they are means for other goals as having wealth. The good human being is a person that desires all real goods but wants the apparent goods to the limit that do not prevent him of having the real good things as health.

The good society is that society that provides real good things for all its members and to prepare the apparent goods for individuals to the extent that having them does not prevent some of the members of society to have the real good things.

The moral virtue is having a habit of desire for real good things and abstaining from desiring things that prevents us from having real good things.

Beauty

Discussion about the truth showed us that we have to make distinction between objective and subjective truths, because the first one is universal and unchangeable but the second one is changeable and is different from one person to another. Also, we said that we should distinguish between truth and taste, and in case of truth, we can solve the disagreements with discussion and reasoning and finally to arrive to agreement, but regarding taste discussion is not useful.

With regard to goodness, we pointed out that it is necessary to distinguish between two kinds of good, real goods and apparent good , and we said that the first relates to our natural and inherent human desires and exists in all human beings alike and therefore they are objective, but the second, is the result of our culture, history and the conditions of the society that we live in, and is different from one person to another. The above discussion makes it clear that real good is truth, but apparent good is taste and as we see, truth dominates goodness.

Beauty is more related to goodness rather than truth, because the goodness relates to qualities and attributes of human beings and beauty is features and qualities of things, and both kinds of those qualities causes us to enjoy and admire them.

Kant, the German philosopher, has the opinion that beauty consists of enjoying by seeing, contemplating or hearing the things without desiring to possess them or interested personally in them as music or painting. Aristotle has the view that beauties that we admire are the things that have order and specified size and also in them coherence and proportions are observed. Beauty is considered mostly subjective because different persons according to their tastes have different judgment about beauty. But since it is possible that experts by examining and discussion about the beauty of a thing agree, therefore we can say beauty also to some extent is objective and at the same time subjective.

Ideas that we use to organize our social, economic and political life: Liberty - Equality - Justice

The above three ideas that our social, political and economic affairs are closely interrelated. In the case of the first three ideas discussed before, we pointed out that truth has sovereignity over the other two and it regulates our thinking about goodness and beauty. Here, in dealing with the second set of ideas, justice has sovereignity over liberty and equality, and with the help of it, we can solve the conflict between equality and liberty whenever it arises.

We should point out that all these three ideas fall in the domain of goodness, because liberty and equality are real good that we need to lead decent human lives in the pursuit of happiness, and also to organize an ideal society in which, happiness and prosperity of all citizens is provided.

However, all real goods are not of equal standing. Wealth and health, for example, are inferior to wisdom. Some real goods are truly good only when they are limited. Pleasure is a real good, but we must not seek pleasure more than we need. The same is true with wealth and both of them are limited real goods. In contrast, knowledge is an unlimited real good. Only justice is unlimited good, but freedom and equality are limited goods.

Some people desire unlimited liberty, but unlimited liberty is in conflict with equality because in this case, some portions of society suffer from serious deprivations. The only equality that these people acquire is the equality of opportunity. They argue that this kind of equality encourages freedom of enterprise. This kind of equality is in favor of those who are bestowed with superior endowments, or attainments and therefore they can make the best of their freedom of opportunity to beat their fellowmen in the race of life. But as a result of this kind of equality, vast inequality of conditions would be created.

On the other hand, there are some persons who are the egalitarians, that not only regard equality of conditions as the supreme value, but they try to achieve it even if that infringes in many ways on individual liberty and initiative, therefore, as we see it, there is a conflict between equality and freedom. The first group giving higher value to liberty and the second group to equality. But if we accept that liberty and equality are only limited good things, and give prime value to justice and not to freedom or equality, then by regulating them by justice, both liberty and equality would be maximized harmoniously and conflict would dissapear.

The justice requires that people have liberty to the extent that does not infringe upon the freedom of others and not create unequal conditions, and as a result of it, the majority of people suffer from being deprived of freedom. Therefore, we conclude that freedom must be to the extent that justice requires.

With respect to equality, justice imposes limitations on the kind and degree of equality. Complete equality is unjust because it limits the freedom of people to benefit from their talents, initiatives and kills incentives of people to do their best for enhancing their societies. As human beings have different endowments, and everybody participates in providing social welfare according to his ability and efforts, therefore, it is necessary that equality be regulated by justice. When justice regulates the pursuit of liberty and equality, both can be maximized harmoniously within the set limits, and the conflict between liberty and equality vanishes. The sovereignty of justice thus corrects the errors, and solves the conflicts.

Different forms of freedom

There are three major forms of freedom. The first is a freedom that is inherent in human nature. We are born with it in our possession, and it is one of the features of human beings, as rational thought and speech that are distinctives of human beings. It is therefore appropriate that we call this as a natural freedom, thus referring to the way in which we possess it. The animals actions and behavior are based on natural instincts, and they do not act consciously or according to their free will, but human beings have freedom to choose or act for themselves.

The second major kind of liberty, is the liberty

that is associated with wisdom and moral virtue. It is possessed only, by those that in the course of their personnel development have acquired some measure of virtue and wisdom, and therefore, we call it acquired freedom.

The third form of freedom is completely dependent on favorable external circumstances. Thus according to the external circumstances sometimes, the people may enjoy it, or be deprived of it, and we call this kind of freedom: circumstantial freedom. The three forms of freedoms are described below:

1- Natural freedom - Our natural freedom of the will is to choose freely. Having such a freedom, our actions are not determined instinctively, or by the impact of external circumstances, as is the case in the behavior of other animals. With this power of free choice, each human being is able to choose what he shall do or shall become. We are free to make oursleves whatever we choose to be. Certainly, the external circumstances may create facilities or hindrances for freedom of the people, and if the limitation is complete then human beings are treated as animals.

2- Acquired or moral freedom - This kind of freedom consists of having a will based on virtue, meaning: a human being with his own will chooses only the real goods i.e., only those things that he really needs, and abstains from desiring those things that are passions, and is injurious to other people or to being good human beings.

Spinoza believes that one of the prisons of humman being is his passions, that is his lower nature. Human moral liberty lies in reason's control of his passions, so that he acquires habits to always make the right choice rather than the wrong choice.

Individuals having the right and freedom to choose and act, therefore, they are responsible for their actions, and for this reason, in different religions, reward and punishments are forseen for good or bad actions. The society also holds its citizens responsible for their action harmful to social interests.

3- Circumstantial freedom - Our circumstantial freedom consists of existence of favorable conditions for carrying out our decision, that we made freely. Of these three major forms of freedom, the only one that needs to be regulated by justice is circumstantial freedom. What one wishes to may be injurious to someone else, or it may be an action in violation of a just law or it may be contrary to the best interests of the community of which the individual is a member. To demand that the scope of one's circumstantial freedom be unlimited is to ask for anarchy and not for freedom.

If an individual lives alone in an isolated island, then it is possible to have unlimited freedom. But in a society, the just limitations of freedom is necessary for protection of rights of other individuals, and is not in conflict with freedom. Freedom to do as one pleases within the limits of justice, is circumstantial freedom.

Living under the constitutional government, the right of suffrage gives individuals a voice, in making the laws and limitations under which they live. They are not subject to the arbitrary rule of a despot, and they are self-governing to the extent, that they are participants in government, and each citizen has a share in sovereignity. In a democratic soviety, all are free men and equal, ruling and being ruled in turn. Slaves do not have political liberty, they are ruled tyranically in the interest of their masters, and not for their own good. Even when people live under benevolent but absolute government, they are not considered as free human beings, but as slaves well fed and looked after.

The unfavorable circumstances are: coercion, constraint, and duress, and in these cases, the people are deprived from freedom to do as they please, by government or some groups of people. The people also may be deprived of having facilities, to be able to use their freedom, such as lack of material living conditions, or education, in this case, they also have no freedom.

The circumstantial freedom to do as one pleases, within the limits, is therefore to be free from coercion, constraint, and duress, and having at one's disposal, the enabling means to act as one wishes. It must be pointed out that not only are we deprived of freedom by unjust laws and arbitrary government decisions, but also, other individuals might infringe upon our freedom, therefore, it is necessary that the government by just laws apply coercive force to secure us from infringements upon our freedom, by other individuals, who would use illegitimate force to interfere with our freedom. But when just laws do not exist or when just laws are not effectively enforced, freedom of the people diminishes; on the contrary, when just laws are enforced, they enlarge the liberty of them.

The maximazation of our circumstantial freedom to do as we please is the great and real "good" conferred upon human beings by just laws, effectiviely enforced. That "good" is further enhanced by just governmnet, which confers political liberty upon all who are entitled to become self-governed, through exercising their suffrage. If the laws of society are not just or government does not put them into action justly, the people would be deprived of freedom and have theright to change government by any means they can.

Certainly, natural and acquired freedom is within our own power, and certainly no organization or society, can confer such liberties to us, or withold them from us. The natural freedom is a "good" conferred on us by God to have a free will or freedom of choice. In the case of acquired freedom, either we acquire or fail to acquire such freedoms, through choices we have ourselves freely made. But circumstantial freedom depends on the conditions of the society that we live in.

The only liberties to which we can make claims upon society, are the freedom to do as we please within the limits imposed by justice that is called political liberty. Whether we have political liberty or not, and the extent to which we have a limited freedom to do as we please depends largely on the society in which we live, its institutions, arrangements, it's form of government and its laws.

The question arises why we are entitled to the rights of freedom, and what is the basis of this entitlement? Answer is that these rights are inherent in our human nature, and it is the duty of a just society to secure them for us, and these rights are inalienable in the sense that a legal deprivation of them must be justified by special consideration.

We are under the moral obligation to pursue happiness, and have a good life and to acquire the real good things, and apparent goods, only to that extent that does not bring injuries, to our having real good things, or to others. The inalienable and natural right to have a good life consists in our entitlement to all the economic goods that we need to sustain our lives, and live well, above the level of mere subsistence, such as health, education, leisure, and so on. To some extent these goods are within our power to provide for ourselves, but some of them only could be provided by society, as facilities for education and healthy environment.

The right to freedom is also indispensable to our pursuit of happiness and well being. But if because of unfavorable social conditions we become unable to choose freely within the limits of just laws, and put in action our decisions, then we have been transformed to the position of lower animals, and not human beings. Therefore, the experts of social sciences have the opinion that in case the government unjustly limits the freedom ot people, the people have the right to regain their freedom by every means even by revolution.

In unfavorable circumstances in a society, nobody, even the virtuous people would not be able to have a good life, because the external factors prevent them from implementing their good decisions.

The different kinds of social freedom and their limitations

The natural freedom of people in a society consists of three groups: political freedom - social freedom - economic freedom. Political freedom: This kind of freedom gives people the right to participate in government and to take part in its decisions. It includes the right to vote, to choose between rival candidates for parliment, and public offices, and to run for those jobs if one so chooses.

Political freedom also includes the right to criticize government policies. People who are politically free can also form and join political parties and associations. This right is called freedom of association.

In the past, many people considered political freedom the most important freedom. They believed that those who are politically free, could vote all other freedoms for themselves. But most people now have the opinion that political freedom means little unless economic and social freedom support it. For example, a person's right to vote does not have much value if he lacks the information to vote in his own behalf.

The societes in which people have political freedom are called democratic societies, and they have the form of republic or constitutional monarchy. In these societies, the people directly or through their elected representatives participate in law making and control carrying out those laws. And the source of sovereignity and government is only the will of the people. In these countries, the arbitrary decisions of a king, or president of the republic, or religious leaders, and so on does not govern the people.

In democratic societies, all people are equal from a political point of view, and everybody rules and is ruled.

In a society, where the people are deprived of political freedom, even if their dictator government is benevolent, the members of that society are like slaves that are well cared for. But they are deprived of a real "good" to which they are by nature entitled, and they can not fulfill all their natural potentialities and talents, and lead full human lives.

Social freedom: includes freedom of speech, of the press, religion, freedom of assembly, academic freedom, and the right to due process of the law.

Freedom of speech includes the right of a person to speak publicly or privately what he believes. And political liberty on the first instance, depends on this right. People inquire, discuss freely and exchange ideas, so that they can decide wisely on political issues. Free speech also enhances political freedom by making government officials aware of public opinion.

Freedom of the press is the right to publish facts, ideas, and opinions without interference from the government, or from private groups. This right includes radio, television, and motion pictures as well as printed material.

Freedom of religion means the right to believe in any religion and to practice it. It also includes the right to have no religion at all.

Freedom of assembly is the right to meet together and to form groups with others of similar interests. It also means that a person may associate with anyone he wishes. On the other hand, no one may be forced to join an association against his will.

Academic and scientific freedom is a group of freedoms claimed by professors, scholars, teachers and students. It includes the right to teach, discuss, research, write, and publish without interference. Academic freedom promotes the exchange of ideas and the spread of knowledge.

Due process of law: a group of legal requirements that must be met before a person accused of crime can be punished. By protecting an individual against unjust imprisonment, due process serves as a safe guard of personal freedom. Due process includes a person's right to know the charges against him. The law also guarantees the right to obtain a legal order. This legal order guarantees that the people not be imprisioned or punished unjustly, and their prestige and property be protected. The people should also have the right to choose an attorney to defend them, and have the right to appeal to higher courts in important matters.

Economic freedom: this kind of freedom enables a person to make his own economic decisions. It includes the right to own property, to use it, and to profit from it. Workers are free to choose and change their jobs. Any person has the freedom to save money and invest it as he wishes. Such freedom forms the basis of an economic system, that is called free enterprise. The basic principle of free enterprise is the policy of "Laisser Faire", which states that the government should not interfere in economic affairs. According to laissez faire, every one would be best off if allowed to pursue his own economic interests withous restriction or special treatment from the government.

Since the 1930's,an economic freedom has come to mean, that everyone has the right to a satisfactory standard of living. This concept of economic freedom, is called freedom from want, and it includes, determination of minimum wages, the hours of work, holiday with pay, and safe working conditions. And if a person is not able to earn a living because of disability, old age, or unemployment, he receives special aid.

Limits on freedom

The laws of any organized society form patterns of balanced freedoms and restrictions. The major reason for restricting freedom, is to prevent injuries to others. To achieve the goal of equal freedom for everyone, government may have to restrict the liberty of certain individuals or groups to act in certain ways, as the law of driving that limits freedom of action of the driver for the safety of the people. Everyone must accept certain duties and responsibilities to maintain and protect society, as the law of paying taxes, or military service.

Limits on political freedom

Democracies divide political power among the

branches of government, between government and citizens, and between majority and minority parties. This division of power restricts various liberties. For example, citizens have the right to vote. As a result, elected officials must respect the voter's opinion. They are not free to govern as they please. A system called the separation of powers divides authority among the three branches of government: executive, legislative, and judicial. Each branch is limited by the other powers. Majority rule does not give the majority party, the liberty to do what ever it wants. No matter how large the majority, it can never take away certain rights and freedoms of the minority.

Limits on social freedom

This kind of limitation prevents people from using their liberty in ways that would harm the health, safety, or welfare of others. For example, free speech does not include the right to shout "fire" in a crowded area if there is no fire. Freedom of speech and the press does not allow a person to tell lies, that damage other people's reputation.

The law also prohibits speeches or publications that would endanger the nation's peace or security.

Also under certain conditons, calling on people to rebel, is forbidden. Government also limits the freedom of press to protect the public morality, i.e., indecent writings and pictures (pornography). The government limits freedom of religion by forbidding certain religious practices., like human sacrifices or polygam, although Islam and other religions permit the practice. Also, in war time, it is possible some kinds of social and political freedoms be limited.

Limits of economic freedom

In the past, most governments put few limits on economic freedom. They followed a policy of not interfering in economic affairs. But since the beginning of the 19th century the development of large scale capitalism, has concentrated wealth in the hands of relatively few people. This development has convinced many persons that government must intervene to protect underprivileged groups and promote equality of economic opportunity. Such beliefs have lead to increased restrictions on big business, and other powerful economic groups. Today in most countries law regulates: wages, hours of work, working conditions, forbid child labor, and even guarantees unemployment insurance. Most people beleive these laws protect economic freedom rather than violate it.

The above discussion shows us that economic freedom today does not have the same meaning as in the past. Today, the main goal of economic freedom is the establishment of full employment, providing health and a minimum standard of living for every one. This kind of freedom is called economic democracy or welfare economics that is complimentary to the political and social freedom. At the present time, most persons believe that without economic democracy, political and social freedom does not have much meaning.

In the year 1941, President Roosevelt declared for all people, four kinds of freedoms that all human beings are entitled to have, and they are as follows: "freedom of speech - freedom of religion - freedom from absolutism and fear - freedom from want."

In 1948, the United Nations general assembly adopted the universal declaration of human rights. This declaration listed rights and freedoms that the United Nations thought should be the goals of all nations. These freedoms includes all kinds of political, social, religious, economic freedoms for all human beings and was approved by all nations.

Limits of religious freedom: freedom of religion is not absolute. If religous practice is injurious to other people, as sacrificing human beings or polygamy, the law prevents it. In communist countries, religious limitation is more extended for all religions. In some countries there is more limitations to minority religious groups.

Limitations of free speech: all societies including democratic ones, put limitations on what people may say. They prohibit certain types of speech that they beleive might harm the government or the people. Drawing a line between dangerous and harmless speech can be extremely difficult. Most non-democratic nations deny freedom of speech to the people. The government of these countries operate under the theory that the ruler or the governing party knows best what is good for the people. Such governments believe that free discussion would interfere with the conduct of public affairs and would create disorder.

Most democratic nations where the freedom of speech is guaranteed, have four major restrictions on free expression:

1- Laws prohibit speech that endangers the privacy

or reputation of individuals.

2- Some laws forbid speech that defends public decency, by using obscenities or by encouraging people to commit acts considered immoral.

3- Laws against spying, treason, and urgin violence prohibit speech that endangers life, property, or national security.

4- Other laws forbid speech that invades the right of people not to listen to it, unless they are invited (as making speech in another party's meeting without permission).

Equality and inequality

The subjects being compared and regarded as equal or unequal fall into two main groups: human beings and all others that includes all the external circumstances under which human beings live and act, or the things two individuals possess or benefit from. We may call the first group as human or personal equality and inequality, and the second, circumstantial equality and inequality.

The personal inequality may arise from the endowments that persons bring into this world at birth or the attributes and skills that they acquire in the course of their lives. The skills might be the work of mind or hands.

Two human beings who start out with equal genetic endowments, and intelligence, may develop their intelligence with different degrees, either through what they themselves do with their minds, or through environmental training and education. Also because the talents, tastes and inclinations of individuals are different from one another, one individual may put his native endowments to work in the production of wealth or other goods, while another, with equal endowments wastes his talents producing nothing.

The personal equality or inequality that arises from the degree to which individuals are natively endowed, is called natural inequality, and inequality of human attainments,we call acquired inequality. All personal equalities and inequalities are either natural or acquired.

Circumstantial inequality may arise from inequality of opportunity or inequality of conditions. The difference between equality of conditions and equality of opportunity can be illustrated by a race in which individuals all start out with equal circumstances. Their equality of opportunity consists of an equality of the conditions, at the beginning under which they begin the race. When the race is over, these same persons may end up with unequal results. Even if we suppose that the two runners had the same endowments, they still might finish the race with unequal results, because one may have had better training and exercise. We call this kind of inequality the "inequality of conditions"

The society may make efforts to grant equality of conditions for all of its members in certain respects as: equal voting rights or equality before the law, equal treatment in the courts, regardless of their inequalities of endowments, or whether they are rich or poor, and so forth.

Equality of conditions may be either an equality in the status granted individuals, equality in the treatment accorded them, or an equality with respect to their possessions of one or another basic human good, such as political liberty, health, schooling, wealth, or healthfull environment. Their equal possessions of such goods depends upon factors controlled by society not entirely by themselves.

The equality or inequality of conditions may be divided in three main categories: political, economic, and social. Equality of opportunity also may be divided similarly in three groups.

Equality of opportunity as we said earlier, is an equality of initial conditions but equality of conditions is the resulting conditions.

Equality that does exist and equality that should exist

When we discuss equality or inequality of persons or conditions, it may be either declarative or prescriptive. To say that two persons are equal in certain respects is a declarative statement but to say that they should be equal is a prescriptive statement.

For example, we can not say that all individuals must be equal in all personal respects, neither with regard to their talents nor with regard to their accomplishments, and all we can say is that one person is equal to another person in one respect and unequal in another respect.

But with regard to circumstantial equality and inequality, we can make both declarative and prescriptive statements. For example, we can say that this group of individuals are equal with respect to a given circumstances, or we can say that they ought to be equal in that respect. For example, in democratic governments, we say that all must have equal rights. But in fact, in some countries like in South Africa, all citizens do not have equal rights (a declarative statement).

We use justice as a regulation only in the sphere of circumstantial equality and inequality, because only there can we make prescriptive proposals, but justice does not enter in the sphere of personal or acquired equality or inequality, where only declarative statements can be made. Personal equality or inequality, natural or acquired is neither just nor unjust, it is only a matter of fact.

Where an inequality of conditions exists but ought not to exist, justice may be required to rectify it by establishing equality in place of inequality, in regards to individuals who make unequal contribution by their work of mind or hand to the national income or welfare, justice may call for unequal rewards that is unequal conditions.

Equality in kind and inequality in degree

To make judgments about, in what cases equality should exist and in what cases it is not desirable, we have to make a distinction between:

A- An equality of conditions that should exist without any difference in degree
B- An equality of condition that ought to exist but should be accompanied by differences in degree, and inequalities among those who are equal in a specified respect. For example, all citizens who have equal voting rights are equal in their political conditions. But when they are divided into franchise as in South Africa, an inequality of political conditions exists. If this is unjust it can be rectified by the establishment of universal suffrage.

When in a country all enjoy an equality in political freedom, it may still remain the case that some citizens elected or appointed to public offices, exercise a greater degree of political power than citizens who do not. Here we have an equality of conditions that is accompanied by a difference in degree. Now if we consider a country that has no universal suffrage, there the population would be divided between those who have political power and freedom, and those who have not, and this is inequality of a kind. In such a country, there will be a second source of political inequality. This time the inequality will occur only among those who have equal in kind, political power, because all have voting rights, but unequal in the degree of political power, some have more of it and some less.

We can summarize by saying that in the sphere of circumstantial equality, equality prevails among those having certain conditions, and inequality prevails between the group that have it and the group that does not have it. We can call inequalities among the haves and have-nots inequality of kind but inequality between have inequality of degree. If all persons are equal in their having the same specific human nature, that is an equality in kind, but one person may be endowed with a specific property to a higher degree than another. The result is an inequality of human beings, all members of the same species but differing from one another as individuals, is an inequality in degree.

In the sphere of circumstantial equality both types of equality or inequality may prevail in fact. All members of a society may be equal in kind, as "haves" in a certain respect, but they may also be unequal in degree in other respects, one having more, the other less.

Those who propose to rectify the injustice of existent inequalities of conditions in the sphere of circumstantial inequalities differ in the proposals that they advance: some propose that, with respect to certain conditions, political, economic or social, all should be equal in kind, without any inequality in degree. All ought to be "haves" with respect to this or that important human good, but among the "haves", none should have more and none have less.

Opposed to them are those who would defend the prespective judgment that, with respect to the same condition, all should be equal in kind, adding that such equality in kind should be attended by inequalities in degree. While all ought to be "haves" with respect to human goods in question, some ought to have more, and some less. We shall attempt to make clear in the following pages which of these two conflicting views is correct.

<u>The equalities to which we are entitled</u>

According to the liberties to which we have a natural right, so it is with some respect to equalities. Justice requires that all be entitled to certain equalities. The ultimate basis of the right, lies in the nature of man.

If human beings were not by nature endowed with freedom of the will and the power of free choice, to be exercised in the pursuit of the ultimate good that they are morally obliged to seek, they would not have, by nature, a right to liberty of action. If they were not by nature political animals, they would not have by nature the right to political liberty. Their right to these liberties lies in the fact that deprivation of them renders their power of free choice ineffective in the pursuit of happiness.

The equalities to which we are entitled, by virtue of being human, are circumstantial, not personal. They are equalities of condition of status, treatment, and opportunity. By being human, we are equal in our humanity. One individual can not be more or less human that another. Some equalities are among the human rights, and all are entitled to have them as equality of conditions of environment, equal treatment, and equality of opportunity.

Certainly, all members of any biological species of living organism, have some properties that are common in many kinds of animals. For example, human beings like other animals have senses and in this respect are like other animals. But some properties are distinctive of the human species that differentiate them from other species, as human's power of speech, free choice, or power of conceptual thought. Therefore, we can not say that one human being is more human than another.

As in the declaration of independence of the United States, this truth is stated as follows: "All men are created equal, and endowed by their creator with certain unalienable rights." All human beings in respect of properties specific to mankind are equal, but from other respects and properties as intelligence, strength are different in degree, all have intelligence and conceptual thought (equality in kind) but some have more and some less (inequality in degree).

Consequently, because of equality of properties in kind, the justice requires establishment of equal conditions in respect to political rights, and equal opportunity and equal treatment for all members of society. Turning now from the political to the economic sphere, parallel reasoning reaches a parallel conclusion: Man has certain biological needs, such as his need for the means of subsistence in order to survive, and his need for certain comforts and conveniences of life, which he needs to live humanly well. Economic goods are the goods that man by nature needs in order to survive and, beyond that, to live well to engage successfully in the pursuit of happiness.

These include more than food and drink, clothing and shelter, they include schooling as instrumental to fulfilling man's need for knowledge and skill, a healthful environment as necessary to fulfilling man's need for health, ample free time needed to engage in playing for the pleasure of it, and in the pursuits of leisure, for the improvement of his mind by engamement in all forms of learning and creative activity. Every human being in entitled to whatever economic goods needed to lead a good life. Therefore, we can say that just all human beings are entitled to a political equality in kind, so they are all entitled to an economic equality in kind.

In both the political and economic sphere, justice requires only as much equality of conditions as human beings have a natural right on the basis of their natural needs.

The above opinion occupies a middle position

between the two extremist views mentioned earlier. At one extreme, the advocates of liberalism maintain that only circumstantial equality to which all human beings are entitled, is equality of opportunity. They argue that more intervention of government in economic affairs will restrict individual liberty of action and freedom of enterprise. At the opposite extreme, the egalitarians maintains that in all respects as in income and wealth ought to be established equality for all men and women.

To our opinion, both views are erroneous and are unjust. Justice requires that all have real goods that human beings are entitled by natural right. But justice also requires that some have more than the others. Those who make more efforts in production of national income have more than the others, in proportion to their efforts.

In conclusion, we can say that justice requires that everybody should have sufficient wealth and income needed for sustaining a good life. If it does not require that all have the same amount. We know that in no country and in no time, all individuals, in political and economic spheres have been completely equal, because the human beings have different degree of endowments, taste and skills.

The inequalities that justice requires to exist

Our discussion here is concerned with a society in which the equality of kind exists, and all members of society different in respect to intelligence and other talents, have political and economic rights, but some have more and some have less. No one should have less than is needed, and no one should have more than is compatible with everyone's having enough. For example, as we mentioned earlier with regard to political power, every one has equal voting power, but some in proportion to their responsibility have more political power. No one should have so great a power to be able to deprive the others from their just political power. Furthermore, having more political power must be legal and vested by the people to them. Having more political power is illigitimate, if it is acquired by some people, through undue influences that they are able to exercise because of their wealth, their social standing, or some other forms of privildeges or prestige.

In the economic sphere, the first principle of justice requires, all must have the economic good as much as sufficient for leading a decent life, and this is the natural rights of all human beings. But the second principle of justice requires that those who have made greater contribution to the production of wealth, are entitled to have more wealth, income and economic goods on two conditions:

1- Nobody in the community must have less than is required for a good life of a human being.

2- Since the amount of wealth available for distribution is limited, no one should be in a position to earn so much wealth, that not enough remains for distribution, in one way or another, that all be able to have enough for a good life.

The first principle requires that every individual have that amount to which all are by natural right entitled. The second principle requires that those who have contributed more to production by their efforts, have more. The two principles are in conflict, but it can be resolved by adding a restrictive qualification to the second. The amount of wealth that any one can justly acquire must be limited so that enough of the finite supply is left for a just distribution in accordance with natural rights.

When the conflict between the two principles is resolved, the result is an economic equality in kind, but inequality in degree. Also, the above principles make it clear that inequality in degree must be based on productive work of mind or hand, and not on illegal activity, like misusing personal or group power or influence.

In a primitive and simple economy, justice requires that every one possess what he produces. But in a complex modern economy, the people produce the goods and services with cooperation and no one produces anything alone. Therefore everybody should benefit justly according to his contribution to the production.

In all circumstances, observance of the two following principles are necessary:

1- Everybody without considering his contribution to the production only because of being human, ought to have the minimum standard of living, for example, sick, old, or disable people.

2- As the supply of goods and services is limited, nobody must have so much that deprives the others of not having enough for having a good life.

As in most countries, the two above principles are usually in conflict with each other. The government fixes limits to wealth and incomes, because justice requires that the first principle that is related to the good living of everyone has priority over the second principle.

The countries that have adopted the above principles in economic regulation of the society are called "welfare states" and their economic system is called "Economic democracy" or "social democracy" or "socialized capitalism."

A just economy, whether achieved by communism (sometimes is called state capitalism) or socialized capitalism (it retains private ownership of capital with some limitations upon it) is one in which no one is destitute, all individuals or families participate in the general economic welfare, in which some have more, because they make more contribution to production.

In countries that have an economic system of extreme liberalism, it is not possible to establish economic democracy, because in these societies, production and distributuion process is wholly in the hands of the private sector. Usually in these societies, the minority of people are very rich but the majority are deprived from having enough to live good.

The societies in which all people have enough to live a good human life, but at the same time, some have more in proportion to their greater contribution to production are called "welfare societies". In welfare states, providing the goods and services necessary for a good life of all citizens is guaranteed by the government. At the same time, the businesses, that private activity in them, is not in conflict with social interests is undertaken by private individuals or companies. In a welfare state, the government guarantees the minimum standard of living for the people who are not able to work. In addition, the government creates equal opportunity for development of the potentialities and capabilities of all members of society, such as education, and full employment.

The domain of justice

We pointed out earlier that the society is organized with the three principles: liberty - equality - and justice, and also, it was shown that justice has sovereignity over the others, and establishes a balance between them. Let us discuss justice:

The domain of justice is divided into two main spheres: One is concerned with the justice of the individual in relation to other human beings, and also, to society and government. The other is concerned with the justice of the state, it's form of government and its laws, its political institutions and economic arrangements, in relation to citizens.

The unjust treatment of an individual in comparison to others is depriving them from their natural rights or real good. Just treatment differs to some extent from fair treatment. Fair treatment is equal treatment between equals and unequal treatment between unequals. Although fair treatment is one of the principles of justice, it is not conclusive, in regards to providing the natural rights of human beings, equal treamnet with all, is required and not equal treatment among equals.

Generally speaking, we can assert that all kinds of damages done by individuals or government to the natural rights of individuals as: harm, beating, imprisonmnet, torture, murder and deprivation of freedom is unjust. On the contrary, the treatment of government or individuals of other persons is in accordance with justice, when it facilitates them in seeking happiness and the good life. Unfair treatment is unfair discrimination between the individuals, as paying women less for equal work, and in this case it is also unjust.

In transaction, the values of the goods that are exchanged is the basis of justice and fairness.

With regard to political, and economic spheres, equality is not the only criterion, because every one must receive his natural rights. In summary, we can say that any kind of violations of rights of others, (government or individuals) is injustice. The natural moral law puts us under the following obligations:

1- To always seek real good and avoid evil, in order to have a good life.

2- To do good and avoid doing evil, meaning acting justly towards others either (a) by not violating their rights and thus not impeding their pursuit of happiness or (b) by treating them fairly in distribution and exchanges.

3- To act for the common good or the general welfare of the community of which we are members. For example, the citizen who commits treason does something against the security and welfare of the state. Likewise, the individual who bribes a public official to achieve an illicit result corrupts the due process of the law and thereby acts contrary to the general interest of the community.

With regard to the just treatment of government, we are chiefly concerned with the justice of it's form, the justice of its economic arrangements, and the justice of its laws and implementation of them.

In the sphere of political institutions, the most just form of government is a republic with universal suffrage, and with a constitution, that includes a bill of economic as well as political rights that secures the natural rights of all. The supreme justice of a constitutional democracy resides in it's distribution of political liberty and equality to all.

In the sphere of economic arrangements, the most just economy is the one that provides all individuals and families with equal participation in the general economic welfare, at least to the extent that all have, the degree of wealth, that is fair, because it gives some "haves" more and some "haves" less in proportion to the contribution they are making in production of of wealth.

The laws are just that protect the natural rights of all citizens and observes justice in distribution of wealth and incomes. The laws are just that:

1- Protect the natural rights of citizens.

2- By legislation safeguards fairness in transactions among individuals.

3- Regulating matters affected with the public interest for the general welfare of the community.

In the next chapter, we are going to discuss in more detail the democratic governments.

CHAPTER 15

DEMOCRACY

Origin of democracy- Democracy began to develop in ancient Greece as early as 600 b.c. The word democracy comes from the Greek words "demos" meaning people and "kratos", which means rule or authority. In ancient times, this kind of government existed in Athens and some other Greek cities. Athenian democracy was a direct democracy rather than a representative one. All citizens participated in government in turn, but the slaves and women were excluded.

In Europe in the middle ages, there was no democracy that existed. There was only a social system known as feudalism. Under feudalism, persons pledged their loyalty and service to one another. Individuals had certain laws which other persons were required to recognize. A feudal court system was established to protect these rights. Such courts led to kings, councils, representative assemblies, and modern parliments.

During the fourteen, fifteen and sixteen centuries, the great cultural reawakening renaissance spread throughout Europe. Consequently, a new spirit of individual thought and independence developed. It influenced political thought and hastened the growth of democracy. People began to demand greater freedom in all areas of life.

The new independence of the individual found religious expression in the protestant reformation. The reformation emphasized the importance of individual conscience. During the early 1500's, Martin Luther, a leader of the reform, opposed the Roman Catholic church as an intermediary between God and man. During the 1500's both Catholics and Protestants defended the right to oppose absolete monarchy. They argued that the political power of earthly rulers comes from the consent of the people.

First in England, democracy was established and gradually strengthened. In 1642, when King Charles I opposed the parliment, a revolution broke up in the country under the leadership of Cromwell, and the king was imprisoned and beheaded. The English revolution finally established the supremacy of parliment. John Locke, the philospher of the revolution declared, "the final authority in political matters belongs to the people." The government's main purpose, he said, was to protect the lives, liberties, and property of the people. Parliment passed the bill or rights in 1689, assuring the people basic civil rights. Only in 1928 were all men and women permitted to vote.

The French contribution to democracy was made in the 1700's by such political thinkers as Montesquieu, Voltaire, and Jean Jacques Rousseau. Their writings helped to bring about the French revolution, which began in 1789. Montesquieu argued that political freedom required the separtion of three branches of government, the executive, legislative, and judicial. Voltaire spoke out against the government's invasion of individual rights and freedom. Rousseau declared in his book the "Social Contract" (1762),"that people have a duty to only obey legitimate powers. The only right rulers have, he added, were those chosen freely by the people.

The United States declaration of independence in 1776, is a classic document of a democratic society. It established human rights as an ideal by which government must be guided. The American constitution divided power between the federal government and the states. The federal power also is divided among the legislative, executive, and judicial branches. Each of the three powers is independent but at the same time, in control of the other two, and so there is a check and balance between the three powers.

In the 19th century, democracy spread to many other countries,and presently, some countries like India chose democracy as a form of government. Democracy did not take root everywhere. Some countries that adopted the constitution later became dictatorships. In Russia, a group of revolutionaries set up a communist dictatorship in 1917 and halted Russia's progress toward democracy. Germany adopted a democratic government in 1919, but Adolf HItler's rise to power brought a fascist dictatorship in 1933. Most governments today claim to be democratic, but many lack the essential freedoms usually associated with democracy.

Many communist governments call themselves "peoples democracies", but the people of these countries are not permitted to criticize the government, nor are they allowed certain basic freedoms, such as freedom of speech and/or freedom of the press.

Definition of democracy

Democracy is a form of government, a way of life, and a goal or ideal. Democracy means rule by the people for the people.

The democracy is in a direct or indirect form. In a direct democracy, the people meet in one place to make the laws for their community. Such democracy was practiced in ancient Athens.

Most modern democracies are a representative democracy. In large communities, it is impossible for all of the people to meet as a group. Instead, they elect a certain number of their fellow citizens to represent them in making decisions about laws and other matters that affect the people. An assembly of representatives is called parliment or congress.

The democratic way of life recognizes the equality and dignity of all persons regardless of race, religion, sex, or social standing. It holds that every one is equal in court trials and other legal matters. It provides freedom of speech, freedom of press, and freedom of religion. The goal of a democratic society is to assure its people of an opportunity to make full use of their abilities.

Democracy in practice often falls short of democracy as an ideal. Nations and governments are classified as being more or less democratic, according to how close they come to the ideal democracy. Most governments claim democracy but are totalitarian. The countries whose governments are in the form of dictatorship of one individual or one party control all aspects of the life of the people.

Aristotle once said: "The basis of democracy is liberty."

Albert Einstein, the great physician has quoted: "My political ideal is democracy. Every one should be respected as an individual, but no one idealized."

Abraham Lincoln has delcared: "As I would not be a slave, so I would not be a master. This expresses my idea of democracy."

Democracy releases the energies of every human being and is the only form of government that is founded in the dignity of man, not on the dignity of some but all men.

Features of democracy

The characteristics of democracies vary from one country to another, but its basic features in most countries are as follows: Freedom of expression: The citizens of a democratic country select their leaders, and influence the policies of their government. For this reason, discussion and understanding of public issues are necessary. To encourage the exchange of ideas, democracy guarantees freedom of speech, the press, and assembly. To have a real democracy, it is necessary that the people have sufficient information about political, social, and economic issues, and this purpose can be achieve only through free speech, discussion, press and other modern communication facilities as, radio and television.

Also in a democratic society, it is important that politicians know how the people feel about public issues, and conform their decisions accordingly if they want to be reelected. The people in a democratic society in seeking support for their own ideas, should respect the rights of others that express different ideas.

Free Elections: In order that people have the chance to participate in government and the government truly represents the people, it is necessary, that elections be held periodically. The possibility of being voted out of office helps and assures that government members pay close attention to public opinion.

In most democracies, the only legal requirements for voting or for holding public office, have to do with age, residence, and citizenship.

The democratic process permits citizens to vote by secret ballot, free from force or bribes. It also requires that election results be protected against dishonesty and fraud.

Majority rule and minority rights - Decisions in a democracy are made according to the majority rule. But a majority rule does not mean that the majority can rule and do whatever it wants. The majority must keep in mind the rights and freedoms of the minority.

Democratic countries guarantee that certain rights can never be taken from the people, even by extremely large majorities. These rights include the basic freedoms of speech, press, assembly and religious worship.

The majority must listen to the views of the minority. The majority should also recognize the right of the minority to try to become the majority by legal means.

Political parties: Political parties are a necessary part of a democratic government. Rival parties make elections meaningful by giving voters a choice among candidates who represent different interests and points of view. Most political parties try to unite as many of these divided interests and opinions as possible through a broad party program. Some countries like the United States and Great Britain have found that a two party system works best in uniting various interests. In a system with more than two major parties, it is more difficult to get and keep a majority rule.

In democratic countries, the parties that are out of power serve as opposition. They criticize the policies and actions of the party in power. In this way, the party in power is called on to justify its actions, and is made responsible to the people. In a totalitarian country, criticism of a party in power, may be labeled, as treason. Often only the "government party" is allowed to exist. Election means little in these countries. The people have no real choice among candidates, and no opportunity to express dissatisfaction with the government.

Division of power: Democratic societies believe it is important to divide and spread out political power. Democracies have various arrangements to prevent any person or branch of government from becoming too powerful. For example, the constitution of the United States divides political power between the states and the federal government. Some powers belong only to the states, some only to the federal government, and some are shared by both.

The constitution further divides the power of the United States government among the President, congress, and the federal courts. No person can serve in more than one of these branches of government at the same time. The power of each branch is designed to check or balance the power of the others. Powers not granted by the constitution to government are reserved to the citizens.

Constitutional government: A democratic government is a government based on law, and in most cases a constitutional government. Constitutions, state the powers and duties of government, and limit what the government may do. They also say how laws shall be made and enforced. Most constitutions include a detailed bill of rights that describes the basic liberties of people and forbids the government to violate those rights.

A constitution may be written or unwritten. The British constitution is unwritten, and it consists of laws passed by parliment, common-law, customs, and beliefs.

Private organizations: In a democracy, individuals and private organizations carry on many social and economic activities that are, for the most part, free of government control. For example, newspapers and magazines are privately owned and managed. Labor unions are run by and for the benefit of workers, not the state. Democratic governments generally do not interfere with religious worship. Private shcools operate along with public schools. Most businesses in democratic societies are privately owned and operated. Great Britain, Sweden, and some other democracies have government ownership and control of certain basic industries and services.

In totalitarian countries, the government alone organizes and controls most associations. The people are not permitted to establish or join most groups without the permission of the state. In such countries as the Soviet Union, the economy is almost completely owned and managed by the state.

Why democracy is preferable to other systems

Preserving human rights: Democracies attempt to preserve individual freedom and to promote equality of opportunity. The United States declaration of independence expressed the belief that "all men are created equal, that they are endowed by their creator with certain unalienable rights, that among these are: life, liberty and the pursuit of happiness." The declaration added that the people may change or abolish the government if it interferes with those rights.

People once thought that the greatest obstacles to individual freedom and equality were political. They believed they could preserve freedom simply by changing the form of government from monarchy to a republic. They claimed that the government that governs least governs best. But in time, many persons became convinced that some government regulation of society and the economy was necessary to preserve personal freedom and equality, as well as to improve the welfare of the nation.

In today's democracies, the government plays an active role in removing inequalities and promoting freedom for all. These nations have programs to provide economic security, to ease suffering, and to develop human potential. Such programs include unemployment insurance, minimum wage laws, old age pensions, health insurance, civil rights laws, and educational aids. Many democracies aim to provide a minimum standard of living and adequate medical care for all. Their goal is not perfect equality, because people differ in ability, and some work harder than others. The goal is equality of opportunity - sometimes called social democracy.

Insuring peaceful change: Those who favor democracy believe that democratic procedures for bringing about change make violent revolutions unnecessary. They claim that democracy meets the just demands of the people more effectively than any other form of government. Supporters of democracy point to the sweeping economic and social changes that have occurred in the United States and Great Britain during the 1900's.

Most of these changes have taken place peacefully, within the framework of existing political institutions.

Democracy also provides for the orderly change and succession of political leaders. Democratic constitutions call for periodic free elections of government leaders. Democracies have an order of succession in case a ruler dies in office or is unable to perform his duties.

Making democracy work

Citizen participation: Democracy calls for widespread participation in politics by the people. It is the duty of all adult citizens to vote in local, state or provincial, and national elections. Qualified individuals should be willing to run for public office, to serve on juries, and to contribute to the welfare of their country to the best of their ability. Citizens should help shape public opinion by speaking out on important issues and by supporting the political party of their choice. An active citizenery is one on the best guarantees against corrupt and inefficient government.

Education and democracy: Widespread participation in politics does not necessarily insure good government. The quality of government depends on the quality of participation. Well informed and well educated citizens are able to participate more intelligently in their government. History shows that democracy is most likely to succeed in countries with high levels of literacy and good educational opportunities. For this reason, democratic governments strongly support education for all citizens.

A democracy needs educated citizens who can think for themselves. Citizens have a duty to take part in public affairs, to keep informed on public issues, and to vote intelligently. Democratic institutions must produce leaders worthy of public trust and responsibility.

In a modern industrial society, a person must have extensive technical knowledge to understand and solve many problems of government. Few voters have either the time or the specialized knowledge for the more difficult problems. Even elected officials are turning more and more to experts for advice. As a result, the voter's role is limited to determining general policy and directions. He does this by making his views known to his representatives, and by voting for candidates who share his views and in whom he has confidence.

Democracy and Economic Development

History shows that the democracy has the best

chance of success in countries that have a stable, growing economy, and few extremes of wealth and poverty. Some scholars believe that democracy works best in countries with a large middle class.

Many democratic governments collapsed during periods of severe economic depression. When large numbers of persons can not find jobs, they are more likely to support groups that want to overthrow the government. To a nation facing possible mass starvation, having enough food may be more important than having voting or other political rights.

Social Mobility

Social mobility is the movement of persons or groups from one class or social group to another. It is vital to democracy. For a person to have a genuine equality of opportunity, he must be able to improve his income, occupation, or social position. A society with a strict class system can not provide the opportunities for individual advancement which democracy calls for. Democracy can not work for example, if some persons are excluded from certain jobs because of their race, religion, or nationality.

Agreement on Fundamentals

Agreement on fundamentals is basic to democracy. A majority of the people in a democracy must believe in the fundamental dignity and equality of all persons.

Although democracy stresses the importance of the individual, citizens must be willing to place the welfare of their country ahead of their own personal interests. The people also must agree on the purpose of government. They will differ on how best to achieve these purposes, but if the purposes and the processes are explicit, then democracy will remain stable.

CHAPTER 16

GENERAL CHARACTERISTICS OF PROGRAMS TO CREATE A WELFARE STATE IN IRAN

Generally speaking, there are two quite different systems of economic development in underdeveloped countries:

A- Economic development on the basis of new colonialism, by imitating the model of western countries:

In this system, the multinational companies, by establishing branches in underdeveloped countries, or participating with internal capitalists, or selling patent rights, create in those countries assembly factories with foreign management and advanced technology. These factories produce consumer goods similar to the goods that are consumed in western capitalist countries for a minority of high income classes in the cities.

With progress of the development process, the countries in question become more and more dependent on foreign countries, for capital goods, raw materials, and technology. Furthermore, the society of these countries loses it's oneness and becomes divided into two seprate societies: one stricly comprised of minority citizens, rich, residing in capital and some big cities, with comsuption pattern, and a way of life similar to foreign industrial countries. The other society comprised of a majority of poor people being employed in agriculture and other economic activities with traditional and prenewtonian technology. The latter society consisting of people with very low incomes, living on a subsistent level, having a very tradional way of life and culture. The two societies have nothing in common and usually despise each other.

Notwithstanding rapid growth of the national income, in these countries every year, the gap between the rich and poor widens, and enmity between privileged and underprivileged people increases, and finally because of universal discontent, the economic growth rate decreases and at the end stops completely.

B- Independent and national economic development for the purpose of providing a good life for all (welfare economic development):

In this system, the main purpose of development is to provide goods and services for all citizens. Social and economic development progress all over the country parallel to each other. The planners choose the technology that conforms with the social and cultural conditions of the country. Agriculture and industries side by side develops and by this progress of development, the country becomes less dependent on foreign countries. As all citizens benefit from the fruits of economic development, they wholeheartedly participate in economic activites and as a result of it, a steady and healthy development goes on for a long time.

By considering our earlier discussion about the economic development of Iran, it becomes clear that in the past, the economic development of Iran was based on the first development system rather than the second one. Therefore a very rapid growth rate, and installation of a great number of factories, dams, roads, airports, ports, hotels and so on, gradually became more dependent on foreign countries;

and inequalities in wealth and incomes increased, resulting in universal discontent and in an uprising of the people.

By keeping in mind the past experiences, we are going to propose a development program based on the second system. The goal of this program would be to transform two societies into one society, provide goods and services required for a good life to all people and make the country more self sufficient and independent.

The program of economic development must establish new order in the country with new values, goals, spirit and moral. The main goal should not be to create a consumption community, but to provide material goods for all, and satisfy the moral and cultural needs of the people. The program primarily must consist of projects for backward areas and distant provinces, so that in a reasonable time all people of the country, economically, socially, and culturally become one society with all having the same desires and ideals and common goals. Also the aim of the plan should be to bring into existence a balanced and democratic community.

The new economic order ought to increase individual freedom and create favorable conditions for developing the abilities and potentialities of all of the people. The program must be initiated by a government freely elected by the people, with participation by all citizens on all levels.

The targets of this program should not be only a quantitative increase of the gross national product, but it's quality and benefits of development fairly distributed among all groups of people. The financial resources of the country ought to be allocated in proportion to the population and needs of all provinces and especially in rural areas.

In the first instance, the primary goal of the program should be the repairing of destructions and ruins caused by the revolution and war of Iran with Iraq, and the elimination of bottlenecks created by an unbalance economy, and transforming two societies to one society.

In this new economic program, industries which use domestic material should be encouraged - and should use capital goods produced internally. Therefore less dependency on foreign countries, which makes them able to stand on their own feet especially if the oil income is decreased.

The government should specify the main portion of infrastructure expenditures to improve the economic and social conditions of rural areas and small towns, such as: construction of roads, schools, housing, pure water, electric and recreation facilities. The government should also encourage small industries, crafts in villages, in order to raise the standard of living in rural areas. This policy would encourage the peasants to stay in villages and produce necessary food for the country.

The plan organization with regards to the transfer of technology from advanced industrial countries should try to choose those technologies that are suitable with conditions of the country, and avoid disruption of the culture and traditions of the country. The habit of economizing ought to be encouraged, and those goods should be produced that are strong and last for a long time, and discourage waste and the throw away policy practiced in western countries, especially in the United States.

The program, in addition to the financial aspects should specify raw materials, services, human skills and machine tools required for implementing each project. In order to avoid inflation and bottlenecks, the government should prepare the accurate amount of physical, human and financial resources of the country. Scarce resources should be allocated to projects before carrying out those projects and if necessary dispense with secondary and ambitious projects.

Here in this chapter, we are going to discuss the main features of the development program that we call the "Independent And National Welfare Program For The People Of Iran".

In the next chapter we will discuss in more detail, the program in various fields of economy: agriculture, industry, mining, services, technology, and the related policies including: commercial, financial, and monetary policies.

In the last chapter, we will discuss the social and political regime within the framework of which our proposed program is most convenient to be carried out.

Absolute growth, even in the western countries has not brought happiness and a good living for all the people.

After the second world war, in all countries (capitalist or communist), rapid economic growth has become one of the most important goals of government. During this period the industrial countries having advanced technology, vast capital, skilled human resource, and favorable social and international conditions, succeeded to achieve great economic successes. Mass production as well as mass consumption and introduction of new goods as television, refrigerator, and so on, enabled these countries to raise the standard of living of their people.

The increase of consumption in industrial countries, in the first instance, is due to two kinds of capitals that nature has put freely at the disposal of these countries: 1- Focil energy, especially oil, that is a non-renewable resource. 2- A natural favorable environment. Unfortunately as human beings, we believe that what we do not produce by labor is free and without value, so the two above mentioned valuable capitals, are considered free and without value. Even Karl Marx in definition of his "value Theory of Labor" has made the same mistake considering non-renewable natural resources as having no value. All the capital created by human labor, as: factories, constructions, infrastructures, etc., are only a small fraction of capital that is used in production. The main part of capital like oil, nature has labored for millions of years to make it, and not the labor of human beings. Because of this erroneous conception, governments after the second world war consumed the valuable natural capital wastefully, and have not made efforts to find substitutes for non-renewable resources before they are exhausted.

In addition to oil, some other resources as iron, chromic and copper, are becoming scarce because their resources is also limited, and at the present rate of exploitation they will be exhausted in a short period and the next generation will be faced with great difficulties. Producing one cadillac car today deprives the next generation from having a tractor for producing food.

The second capital that nature has bestowed freely is a favorable natural environment. But the countries especially advanced industrial countries (capitalist or socialist), in the last three decades, have polluted it in many ways. For example, pouring the chemical wastes of factories in the rivers and seas, and especially by developing the production of atomic energy, the pollution of the environment has increased immensly. In most industrial countries, wastage, pollution of the air, and water has seriously endangered the health of the people. About 25% of the waters are polluted, and as a result of pollution, many kinds of diseases as cancer, heart attacks and psychic diseases have increased.

The United States having only 6% of the worlds population consumes alone more than one third of the worlds energy and raw materials. It is estimated that every American uses about 20,000 kilos of mineral products in one year.

It is estimated that at the present level of rate of increase, the world population would reach 6 billion in the year 2000. Taking into account the present growth rate of industrial and underdeveloped countries, the consumption of energy and raw materials and food would be four times greater than the present. Consequently, if underdeveloped countries decide to increase their consumption to the level of industrialized nations, by the first decade of the year 2000, they would not be able to procure energy and raw materials needed for this purpose.

Ghandi, the great leader of India once said, "The world's resources is only sufficient to provide the real needs of human beings and not their passion and desires."

In the United States of America, 600,000 tons of aluminum, 400,000 tons of other metals, 13 million tons of glass, 500,000 tons of paper, 17 million tin boxes, 38 billion bottles, 7 million television, and 7 million cars are disposed of as waste materials. That is why Galbriet, the economist and Noble Prize winner stated in his book called "The Problems Of An Opulent Society": "Instead of calling this age an atomic or space age, we must call it "The Throw Away age."

In capitalist industrial countries, the companies produce goods that in a short time become obsolete. Furthermore, they encourage the people by way of advertisements to follow the new models and to change old models every year. In packaged foods, they add so much chemical materials, that no one knows what he is consuming, food or chemicals.

The citizens of the United States usually use one fourth of their income for transport and buying cars, and every year about 55,000 persons are killed by car accidents, and more than 5 million people injured. In the cities because of air pollution, the health of the people is faced with real danger. There is also no security in the cities and people do not dare to walk even in the daytime in the streets.

They call the streets "drive" meaning that they are only for driving and not walking.

During the 1970's, the industrial world was faced with an intense crisis. Notwithstanding the considerable improvement of the material conditions of the people, in those countries, crime, violence, suicide, divorce and family breakups are increasing greatly, and most people are indifferent to moral values, so that it is not certain, what is good and what is bad. Extreme freedom of sex, has increased the number of homosexuality in the cities and families are constantly threatened.

In the 1970's, the monetary and exchange system of these countries weakened, and inflation together with unemployment occurred in all western countries that had created great discontent among the people.

Due to the above facts, today, most people are questioning that only absolute material growth and increase of consumption is sufficient to make people happy and lead a good life. Gradually, some people in these countries are again attracted by moral concepts and a desire to live a simple and natural life, for example, some people are using bicycles instead of cars, and prefere to live in the countryside rather than in towns.

Iran should not imitate the economic development of capitalist industrial countries.

The past economic development experience of Iran, shows us that in this country, the absolute growth of western countries is not only capable of eliminating poverty, backwardness and the resolution of acute social problems, but it creates new serious political and social problems and destabilizes the society.

As we said earlier in this book, this system of development transforms the society into two separate societies: one society composed of the upper stratum of citizens of big cities, with a modern economy and consumption similar to that of foreign countries, and the other consisting of a majority of people with a traditional economy living on a subsistent level. The absolute growth is beneficial to a minority group of citizens of the country, and creates dualism of the economy, society and culture, that coincides with dualism of income and wealth.

Furthermore, this kind of development makes the country more dependent on foreign countries and creates high inflation and unemployment, and disrupts the culture and values and traditions of the country. The integration of two separate societies in Iran that has been the result of past economic development policies, ought to be the most important goal of economic development in the future. This purpose could be achieve only by suitable policies that eliminates great differences in wealth and incomes, and not by pursuing growth on the model of western capitalist countries.

The criterion for the quantitative figures of the Gross National Product, investment and savings usually employed in industrial countries, are irrelevant to the underdeveloped countries like Iran. Therefore, instead of the maximization of the Gross National Product and growth rate, there should be the maximization of the welfare of all groups of people and full employeemnt of human resources should be the primary goal of economic development in Iran.

Also the aim of economic development should not be only the material well being of the people, the creation of a consumer society, increase of demand for luxury goods, as in western countries, and substitute pyschic desires by advertisement to the real needs of the people. The experience also shows that consumerism has very bad effects on the moral behavior of citizens, because it encourages prodigality, waste of resources (throw away policy). pleasure living, corruption, bribery and crime. The aim of the economic and social development should be to substitute the spirit of duty and moral virtues to the spirit of consumerism and materialism. In consumer societies, the individuals ambition is satisfied only by more consumption and showing luxury living to others. Furthermore, underdeveloped countries imitating the way of life of foreigners, results in foreign domination of the national culture, and values. At the present, the dominance of underdeveloped countries by industrial countries is not only political but military and cultural as well, and is usually called neocolonialism. Usually the upper classes of people of underdeveloped countries not only imitate the consumption habits but also the lifestyle of dominant countries, isolating them from the majority of people in the country. In addition, scarce resources of the country are used to prepare luxury goods for the minority of rich people.

From the above discussion we conclude that, in Iran, the goal of development should not only be to produce more goods but also to cultivate a quality of life and moral virtues. People need kindness, friendship, respect, freedom, personality, and time for leisure and cultural activities. One of the goals of economic and social development should be the establishment of security (economic, political and judicial), belonging to the community, participation and cooperation in decision making in all spheres, providing social justice, and creating opportunity for every one to develop talents and abilities, and a healthy natural and social environment.

In the above mentioned development system that we may call a "welfare state system", the aim is not to increase the wants of the people, but with minimum consumption to maximize welfare and provide good living for all, and the remaining time of citizens to be used for physical exercise, improving health of the body and spirit, purifying moral behavior, and cultural creativeness.

In addition, this way of life with moderate consumption, would prevent the people from 'literally cutting each others throat', and create affection and kindness among the people, and makes the people and the country become more independent and self sufficient.

Some economists believe that the development is

accumulating capital and wealth, but this traditional concept of development, history shows everywhere that failure is inevitable. Today most economists believe that development, encompasses the potentialities of the people, especially their education. They argue that the development process can only be achieved by trained and skilled hands and minds, and by efforts of the people that have confidence in themselves, and are able to distinguish their needs, and know how to satisfy them, without the help of foreigners.

The needs of the people that economic development should provide for are: food, habitation, health service, transport, clothing and education. The resources of the country should be earmarked for providing these goods and services.

Development activities should be enacted with the participation of all people, where they live

If it is accepted that real development is the development of creative power and abilities of the people, then it has to be put in action where the people are living, in order that all citizens of the country could participate actively in carrying out the developmental projects.

The people should be encouraged to prepare themselves with the projects for providing their needs, and implement it with the support of the government within the framework of the national general plan. Therefore, it can be said that real development is to "become" and not to "have".

In democratic societies, all decisions for economic development should not be taken by the above authorities. Each group of people from the village level on, should try to solve their problems themselves. Certainly, the problems that are related to a greater community or the whole nation have to be handled by upper authorities, but also in these cases, it is necessary to consider the views of those whose destiny is affected by these decisions. Government should provide facilities required, in order for the people to accomplish their duties.

Democratic decision making, in all levels is of primary importance for the system of welfare economics, that is based on producing the goods and services that all people need, and this program should be enacted in: factories, schools, villages, towns and all government institutions. One of the best ways to achieve this purpose is to encourage and support the establishments of the councils of workers, farmers, and government employees, etc.

In economic affairs, in order to safegauard the interest of underpriviliged people, intervention and control of the government is necessary.

Growth together with distribution should be the goal of development

The absolute growth alone will not solve the poverty and the problem of backwardness. On the contary as experience shows, it widens the gap between the rich and the poor. Therefore, a harmonious development program to increase production with a just distribution among different groups of people, should be taken into consideration. The program should clearly show what effects it would have in eliminating the inequalities of wealth and incomes, and what groups would benefit from the fruits of development.

In Iran, distribution of wealth is more unequal than income, and government policy in past development plans intensified this unfavorable condition. Income inequality in Iran is primarily due to inequality of wealth, skill and lack of educational opportunity for the majority of the people.

The primary strategy in formulating a development plan should be to specify a great portion of investments to such projects that increase incomes of low income groups and their access to infrastructure, public utilities, such as: roads, electricity, health services and education etc. Contrary to the past policy, that neglected rural areas and small towns, in the new economic social order, these areas should have priority in allocation of investment funds.

Education and training of people should be the primary goal of the development process

The main cause of Iran's backwardness is not material poverty, It is due to the shortcomings of the educational system and a shortage of skilled labor, specialists and also a lack of an honest and efficient administration.

Real development is not only increasing the number of factories and construction of hotels, and producing more material things, it is primarily, creating a favorable environment for educating and training the people with good character, discipline and self confidence to be able to use their abilities for improving their own economic and social conditions.

Information and statistics needed for preparing an economic program

In previous years in Iran, the Central Bank and Plan Organization collected and published statistics and information about the growth of different sectors of the economy neglecting facts about the increase of income of different areas and different groups of people, which is required for our proposed welfare economic development program. The information gathered showed only the statistics of the modern sector and not the traditional sector of the economy.

Before formulating a development program, it is necessary to provide complete information about the national income, employment and other necessary statistics in both a modern and traditional sector of the economy. The plan organization should clearly and separately publish what effects this program would have in different areas and different groups, wealth and income. The plan should show how scarce resources of the country are. The economic activity in different sectors should be divided into: small, middle and big. With regards to wages and salaries, it is advisable to divide them into three categories: upper, middle and lower classes.

In addition, it is essential to determine the factors that influence incomes, employment, demand for goods and services, and domestic products.

In summary, we believe that the following information and statistics are necessary for preparing the new economic development program:

1- The quantity and quality of modern and traditional production sectors should be shown separately.

2- Employment opportunity in the different sectors: industries, agriculture, services, small industries, crafts, self-employed, and professions. The income level of each sector should be gathered and published separately.

3- Information about the conditions of distribution of wealth and ownership of properties, land and businesses in the country.

4- The rate of increase of population in towns and rural areas.

5- The amount and sources of incomes including: profit, interest, rent, salary and wages.

6- The statistics of the goods that are consumed by the producers themselves without coming to the market.

In summary, we confirm that the welfare development program is indispensable. Growth and distribution should be taken into account and the following points should be observed:

1- Economic and social groups of the country should be specified, in order for the government to determine appropriate policies.

2- The primary aim of economic policies should be to close the gap between low and high income groups.

3- Government should allocate the main part of infrastructure and public services expenditrues to backward areas.

CHAPTER 17

THE PROGRAMS FOR DEVELOPING VARIOUS ECONOMIC AND SOCIAL SECTORS IN IRAN

Agriculture

One of the main shortcomings of the economic development in Iran in previous years was the low growth of the agricultural sector, in comparison with other sectors. The shares of agriculture in the national income that was 30% in the year 1962, had fallen to only 10% in 1977, a year before the revolution. As a result of the population increase, and rise of income of the people, growing industries, demand for food, as well as raw materials required by industries increased sharply.

Consequently, the agriculture of Iran in the year 1962,(the net exporter) earned a considerable amount of exchange for the country, and in recent years, it has been transformed to a net importer, and large amounts of the oil income is used to finance food imports, as well as raw materials. The country has become dependent on foreign countries for its food and raw material requirements.

Furthermore, due to great differences of incomes between rural areas and towns, (in the year 1962 the proportion was 1 to 2 but in the year 1977 changed to 1 to 8) to the disadvantage of rural areas, and for lack of facilities for a decent life, health service, education, employment opportunity, the peasants have endlessly emigrated to towns. The population of big cities especially Tehran has increased to such an extent that today they are faced with acute problems such as housing, water, eletricity and transport.

The low growth rate of agriculture in Iran is primarily due to the neglect of the government in the last 15 years to consider development plans for this sector, high priority. Credits earmarked for agriculture in the plans were insufficient and small in proportion to it's importance in the economy of the country. Government also fixed low prices for agricultural products through subsidizing imported food products, and as a result of this policy, the agricultural activity became an unprofitable economic activity.

The private sector, due to the shortage of water in Iran and the existence of great distance between villages, had no incentive to invest in agriculture. After the land reform, the government who had replaced the land owners, had the duty of providing sufficient investment funds for farmers, and also to create necessary facilities to transform agricultural acitivity to profitable economic activity.

Unfortunately the government neglected to allocate sufficient investment funds for agriculture and this had been on of the factors that hurt the agricultural field.

To compensate for the past wrongs, the government should consider agricultural development as having the first priority in allocating investment funds and credits. Considering the increase of the world's population and shortage of food - production in most countries and increase of Iran's population in the future, the Iranian government should do it's best to make the country's food production and consumption self sufficient as much as possible. The oil resource that is the national capital, and today used to finance food and other consumption imports, should be used only to import capital goods for economic development. We have to bear in mind that, in a short period of time, it is always possible to meet the shortage of food products by imports financed by the oil income, but in the long run when the oil resources are exhausted, the country will face many problems.

The policy of agricultural development should be based on the encouragement of decentralized farming, using simple and cheap technology. Too much mechanization and automation is not advisable, because it creates unemployment in the rural areas. Government should provide agricultural tools, water, better seeds, know how, and training facilities. Experience shows that it is better to use less natural fertilizers and insecticide to insure healthy produce. In many countries in recent years, organic farming has proven to be preferable, for the reasons that, it uses less energy, pollutes less environment, but at the same time, it's nutritious value is greater than non-organic cultivation.

Creating rural industries with cheap and simple technology is essential for agricultural development, because employment in small industries and crafts as secondary jobs raises the incomes of peasants and encourages them to stay in the countryside and produce necessary food for the country. Also it is required to encourage the cooperation and participation of peasants to build schools, roads, houses and other public utilities with the help of government.

In the agricultural development policy, it is useful to study and follow the experience of India, because of India's very large population and limited resources. In the past years, India was forced to import a considerable amount of food products from abroad, but in recent years, it increased immensly it's agricultural production, by way of using cheap and simple agricultural tools, as well as cheap energy and has been successful in becoming self sufficient in food producing. India has installed in each village, a gas plant for the purpose of transforming the animal waste into fertilizer and a small plant to transform sunlight to electric power. This country until the present time has established about 400,000 such plants in rural areas.

Because of Iran's similarities to India, the government should organized a study group to research India's experiences, and prepare a program suitable to the conditions of Iran.

To improve the agricultural conditions in Iran, the following actions are required to be taken by government:

1- Completion of land reform, so that each farmer owns the land that he cultivates.

2- Create agricultural cooperatives for the purpose of production, and providing credits, fertilizers, better seeds, machine tools, and selling the products. The group production should be encouraged in order to avoid the allotment of lands to smaller portions.

3- Allocation of sufficient credits by government to all farmers for the purpose of providing fertilizer, better seeds, agricultural tools, and construction of schools, roads and so on.

4- Providing sufficient water through constructing dams, and kanats, and organizing an efficient watering system.

5- Installing technical aid and training centers in rural areas, and acquainting the peasants with the best farming practices and helping them in fighting against insects and pests.

6- Establishing special research centers for recognizing the features of water, soil and climate of different areas, and specifiying what kind of cultivation is suitable for each area, and putting the result of researches at the disposal of the farmers.

7- Improving the cattle breeding and increasing poultry production.

8- Fixing the minimum prices for agricultural products, at a level that farming activity becomes profitable and peasants could have a standard of living comparable with other laborers.

9- Limiting the imports of food products and granting subsidies to domestic producers similar to imported products.

10- Creating secondary jobs for peasants by encouraging rural industries and crafts in order to increase rural incomes.

11- Construction of rural roads and carrying out special projects in order to provide public services for peasants such as: educational facilities, health centers, house building, agricultural insurance and social security.

12- Increasing the farming productivity and extension of surface of cultivation in the country.

13- Establishment of prizes for the farmers that produce better quality, and more farm products.

Industrial development and creating healthy industries

Keeping in mind that the oil reserves are limited and would be exhuasted in the near future, and acknowledging that oil is a natural endowment that belongs also to other generations, is the moral duty of government and the people of Iran, thus creating basic industries and a genuine economic development to provide posterity with benefits from the results of the oil investments.

Considering the above facts, the industrial policy of the government should insure that the oil is utilized to create such industries that in the future could replace the oil industry.

The industrialization of Iran is required not only to raise the standard of living of the people, but also to produce the needed consumer goods at home, as well as exporting some portion of its products to earn sufficient foregin exchange for financing imports of capital and other essential goods in the future. History shows that the country that produces only agricultural products, raw materials, and whose exports consist of limited number of farm produces and raw materials, is in a very weak position especially when there is worldwide depression in international markets. In addition, such a country does not enjoy economic independence.

The policy of industrialization should be so formulated that it generates equal opportunity for all citizens, and in a reasonable time makes the country self sufficient from an industrial point of view.

To achieve these goals, it is recommended that the following points are taken into consideration in preparing an industrial program:

1- The industrial projects should have priority in producing the essential wants of the people and not luxury goods for the minority rich persons.

2- Government's investment ought to be earmarked for basic industries, as iron mill, machine making, petrochemical as well as infrastructure including dams, electric power, energy, road, railway, education, health, communications and so on. The infrastructure spending should not be allocated to the cities only, it must be distributed all over the country giving priority to rural and backward areas, in order to reverse the past policy and eliminate the economic and social dualism in the country.

3- The project's priority should be to employ raw materials produced at home, or those industries that in a short time could be able to compete with similar foreign goods, and by exporting some part of their products, earn enough foreign exchange to finance their requirements of capital goods and raw materials.

4- Intensive labor, small industries, and handicrafts should be encouraged, in order to eliminate unemployment and avoid concentration of industries in some areas. In addition, small industries make the country technically less dependent on foreign countries, and is conducive for having a healthy environment.

5- The protection policy of industries should be moderate, temporary, exactly calculated, beginning from the highest level, decreasing gradually and stopped a predetermined time, and government controlled, in order not to exploit the consumers and the establishment of unhealthy industries that can never stand on their own feet without the aid of government.

6- A maximum amount of protection should be given to those industries that produce essential goods, use domestic raw materials and create a maximum amount of jobs.

7- Protection of existing assembly plants should be proportionate to the value added to the product in the country and not to the total value of the finished product, in order that these industries be encouraged to produce domestic products gradually and allow the assembly plants to become real national industries.

8- The private sector should activate in industries within the framework of the general economic plan. The quality of their products, prices, and profits should be controlled by the government for safeguarding the interests of consumers. Private industries should benefit from the same kind of facilities that similar governmental industries enjoy, in order that fair competition exists between them, and the efficiency and profitability of governmental industries increases.

The kind of technology Iran needs

Science and technology in the last three centuries, have been the most important factor for the progress of human beings, and in advanced countries, have freed the people from toil, hunger and diseases. If the underdeveloped countries choose the techniques that are in conformity with their conditions, they could enjoy the same benefits. The country that dispenses with modern sciences and technology is condemning millions of its citizens to permanent poverty and hunger. The country of communist China, after the revolution, notwithstanding great efforts of the people, for decades, because of backwardness in sciences and technology, it was capable of avoiding famine, but remained backwards until the present time, The standard of living of its people existed on a subsistent level.

On the other hand, the underdeveloped countries like Iran should not use the same technology that is suitable to the conditions of the advanced industrial countries. Experience in previous years in Iran shows that it creates unfavorable side effects, such as unemployment, inequality in wealth and income, pollution of enviornment, and so on.

The defects of technology of Iran in the past

In the last two decades, Iran imported capital intensive and complex technology from capitalist western countries through bilateral agreements, and at the present, it is highly dependent economically and technologically to those countries. These technologies are created for the requirements of advanced industrial countries and not Iran. Consequently, the economic development of Iran imitating the model of advanced capitalist countries, and using capital intensive and complex technology, has created many unfavorable effects on the country's economy and society, of which the most important are: unemployment, inequality of incomes and wealth, dualism economy, and dependency on foreign countries.

The defects of capital intensive technology

The capital intensive and complex technology makes the country permanently dependent on foreign countries for import of machines, raw material, semi-finished goods and know-how. The country should pay every year great sums to foreigners for buying patent rights. In addition, this kind of technology increases profits of capital, income of specialists, engineers and skilled workers to the disadvantage of unskilled workers. It also changes the pattern of consumption and concentrates the economic activities in big cities and as a result, the society is transformed into separate societies with different standards of living, culture, and way of life.

Capital intensive technology also encourages the students to have university degrees, and these students after finishing their post graduate studies leave the country, and stay permanently in foreign countries. Finally this kind of technology requires a great amount of investment for creating infrastructure and construction of roads, railroads and communications. Even in western industrial countries, automation and capital intensive technology has increased productivity, at the same time, it has increased unemployment, and has transformed work to a boring and monotonous activity. In these countries, boring and monotonous work in big factories has ruined the spirit of workers. Human beings enjoy work and lead happy lives when both their hands and minds are used in work. The other disadvantage of capital intensive technology is that it pollutes air, water and ruins the environment.

Labor intensive and medium technology is preferable

Underdeveloped countries like Iran should choose technology that conforms with the conditions of the country and would not have unfavorable effect on culture, traditions, and moral values of the country, and enables the people to reach their full potential. The technology should be democratically fair making production by a mass of people instead of "mass production with few people".

In our view, the appropriate technology for Iran should be labor intensive in a medium range, because it creates full employment, makes the country self sufficient in agriculture, and prevents the cities from becoming too big, decreases inequality and dependency on foreign countries.

In small labor intensive industries usually the work is not boring and dull, and human relations between workers and employers is very pleasant. In big capital intensive industries the employers considers the workers as machine tools that produce goods of better quality, transforming the human beings to creatures of low standing, quality and spirit. Therefore, even in advanced industrial countries, the economists and sociologist have the opinion that technology should become in those country, simpler, cheaper, and factories smaller and healthier, so that the machines serve the employees instead of the workers being subservient to the machines.

Generally, small factories and plants have the following advantages:

1- They use less resources.

2- They pollute less environment.

3- They are more suitable for decentralized production and as a result of it, there would be a better balance in distribution of population between towns and rural areas.

4- The people would be able to produce their needs where they are living without being in need of foreign specialists, and so the capital would be available for use by the people.

5- The small machines create a better human relationship and as a result, the contrast between economic progress and moral values disappears.

Especially for agricultural development, it is essential to choose carefully the techniques that have no undesirable effects on family life, rural traditions and values. The experience of India is very useful to imitate. Iran like that country, by using simple and cheap technology would be able to provide energy, water, small industries, and handicrafts and other facilities for peasants. Furthermore, this policy encourages the peasants to stay in villages and produce sufficient food for the country.

The policy of government should be to produce capital goods in the country, but this is possible only when the technology is simple and does not require foreign skill and materials.

Certainly, some basic industries as oil refineries or petrochemical companies require complex and hig technology that should be imported from advanced industrial countries, but in this case, the government should make arrangements to train Iranians to acquire the necessary know-how.

In choosing the technology for the economic development of Iran, the four following points should be taken into consideration:

1- Plants and production units to be installed in all areas where the people live and not concentrated in big cities.

2- Technology should be simple without the need of high skills, and labor intensive, the factories should be small, especially in industries that produce essential goods for people, as food, clothing, housing.

3- Technology should be cheap and enable the people to make machines and tools domestically.

4- Technology should utilize domestic raw materials.

We believe, by observing these principles in choosing technology, the contrast between economic progress and moral values, and national culture that has occurred in previous years in Iran, because of imitating most advanced countries in using capital intensive and complex technology would be eliminated, and the material welfare of the people as well as the spiritual and moral health of the people would be fulfilled.

Certainly, as we pointed out earlier, some basic industries need a capital intensive and complex technology that is excluded from the above considerations.

The main purpose of development should be: the country, as soon as possible, become independent from an industrial and technological point of view. For achieving this purpose, it is essential for that country to create a national technology by encouraging scientists, researches and strengthening research centers and universities as well as technical institutions and induce the industries to establish close relations with those establishments.

How to use foreign technology

The international cooperation in the field of technology and science is essential for underdeveloped countries like Iran in order to benefit from the fruits of progress of sciences and technology of the world. No country alone can solve all of the problems of technology. Japan considered today as one of the most industrialized countries of the world, borrowed the main part of it's technology from western countries, but this country adopted foreign technology so well, its conditions and culture, that today it has become one of the strongest competitors of western industrial countries.

In Iran, the government should control the transfer of technology from foreign countries to Iran, in order that only those technologies that are appropriate to the conditions of the country be used in industries. For this purpose, we recommend that the government establish a special institution to study the foreign technologies and allow those technologies to become national with no unfavorable effects in the country's society and culture.

In Iran, there is no close contact between, universities, research centers and industries. One of the reason for this shortcoming, is that most researches and studies in universities are academic and not practical in industries and also because the industries use foreign technology and foreign sepcialist, therefore, they do not feel the need for domestic technological research centers. But in the future, if we are going to have a national technology, it is necessary to establish close relations between industries and universities and research centers. For this purpose, it is urgent to establish a center to incorporate and make practical the technological findings of universities and research centers and to organize seminars between industrialists, scientists and researchers, and give advise in technical matters to industrialists.

Furthermore, Iran should exchange views with other underdeveloped countries,like India,regarding the transfer of technology and cooperate with those countries in the fields of research in industrial engineering, electronics, rural industries, fertilizers, energy and consumer industries. The underdeveloped countries should make efforts to establish a union strong enough to be able to conclude favorable relation with advanced industrial countries.

The Energy Policy

Providing sufficient energy and fuel,domestically, is a basic condition for economic progress of a country and it's economic and political independence. Presently, the most important source of energy and fuel in Iran is oil, but as we know, the oil reserves of Iran are limited. Considering the country's energy possibilities, the government should base it's energy policy on varied sources of energy. The various sources of energy of Iran are discussed as follows:

1- Oil

The economy of Iran after the second world war, gradually became dependent on oil. This dependency continued to grow every year so that in 1977, (the year before the revolution), the oil sector comprised 40% of the Gross National Product, 77% of the government's income and 90% of the foreign exchange earnings of the country. The income of the country from the oil exports before the revolution was about 20 billion a year.

Although oil provides valuable possibilities for economic development in the country, it creates other limits for the economy. For example, the oil industry is the capital, skilled intensive, and highly automized, so it creates a small number of direct jobs. In addition , injection of the oil income into the domestic economy intensifies inflation, and encourages the establishment of unhealthy industries that are only dependent on the oil income. It also expands the service sector of the economy, and unproductive activities as speculation in land transactions. The oil income makes the incomes more unequal, and a considerable portion of the oil exchange earnings usually is used to finance the import of luxury goods for the upper classes of society. All these factors prevents the steady, healthy and continuous growth of the economy.

In Iran, in previous years, oil has been wrongly considered as income. It is not created by human labor, it is the endowment of nature to be consumed not only by one generation, but all posterity.

The economic policy of the country in the future regarding oil, should be based on oil exploitation only to the amount that is required for imports of capital goods for the purpose of establishing basic industries that in the future can be a substitute to oil, and also necessary infrastructure. In reasonable time, the government should endeavor to become self-sufficient, in food and raw material production, as well as consumer goods, and should discourage the installation of industries that are dependent on oil for importing raw materials or semi-finished goods, so that gradually the economy of the country becomes less dependent on oil.

It is estimated that Iran's oil production and export would gradually decrease in the decade of 1990, and later the exports would stop. According to the views of some experts, Iran has only 25 years to do without oil, therefore, they recommended that the country find other resources for the country's energy requirements, and use oil as raw material for petrochemical industries, and export, for financing imports for capital goods.

During the revolution, investment for reexploitation of the oil wells, and exploration of oil reserves and construcion of new refineries,as well as protection of oil installations decreased sharply. In addition, the war with Iraq caused great damages to Abadan refinery, and also other oil installations. The neglect of government during this period caused some part of the oil reserves to be lost forever.

It is urgent that the government allocate sufficient investments in the future to repair the damaged installations - for constructions of new refineries, exploration of oil and injection of gas to wells in order to revitalize the reserves of the old oil wells.

2- Gas industry and energy

The prospect of natural gas is better than oil in Iran. According to the recent estimation of the experts, Iran's gas reserves are about 10,600 billion cubic meter, and the country ranks second in the world to the Soviet Union, and possesses more than 20% of the world's gas reserves. It is estimated that at the present rate of production, the gas reserves of Iran will meet the internal consumption and exports for 250 years.

The exploitation of gas for domestic consumption and injection into oil wells, as well as, raw material for petrochemical industries and export for the purpose to procure foreign exchange to finance imports, is necessary. It is highly recommended that the government allocate in future programs, adequate amounts of funds for investment in gas production and distribution.

The main part of Iran's gas reserves is mixed with oil, and in the past, it was burning in flames and wasted. Before the revolution, the government made efforts to prevent the waste of gas and put into action a program that in 1980 prevented the burning and waste of gas. After the revolution, this program stopped altogether and again the gas mixed with oil burned with flames and is wasted. It is essential that in the future, the program of preventing gas from burning in the production of oil continue. Using gas as energy for domestic consumption, not only provides clean fuel, but it is also economically advantageous. Injection of gas to oil wells is also required to increase oil production in the future.

Iran has concluded an agreement with Russia in previous years, to export gas to that country and has spent immense amount of money to build pipelines all over the country. The conditions of the agreement, especially the price determined for the gas is not economically profitable for Iran. The agreement expires in 1985 and it is necessary to revise the conditions if Iran's favor in renewing this agreement.

Utilizing the gas internally is very advantageous for the country, because it is cheaper, cleaner and more abundant in comparison with other energy resources, but it also frees the oil to be exported or used for other purposes. The main disadvantage of gas, is the vast amount of investments needed for constructing pipelines, throughout cities and the danger of gas explosion. Therefore, some countries like West Germany, having spent in the past, billions of dollars for constructing the pipe lines, at the present, are trying to transform gas in special centers to electricity and they transfer electricity to the cities for consumption. Since Iran has not yet built pipelines for gas transportation in most towns, it is advisable to study this project to find if it is economically feasible.

In villages with vast distances between one another, instead of constructing pipe lines, it is economical to put at the disposal of peasants, liquid gas in capsuls of 12 kilos.

3- Hydroelectric power

The prospect of hydroelectric power is bright in Iran. At the present, 23% of the country's electric consumption is provided by dams that produce hydroelectric power. In the future, it is estimated that the main part of the hydroelectric power would be produced by waters of rivers that originate from the Zagros mountains, to the Persian Gulf, and to the the rivers that originate from Alborz mountains and join at the Caspian sea. The experts have the opinion that by building small dams in appropriate places on those rivers, a considerable part of the electric power, as well as sufficient water for farming would be provided for the country.

4- Traditional electric power

About 56% of the electric power of the country is produced by gas, and diesel turbins. The electric producing factories in Iran even before the revolution were in bad condition, but after the revolution, because of the shortage of necessary tools and specialists that left the country, their conditions worsened, so that at the present, some of them are producing electricity at a very low capacity and some others are standing idle.

In the future, the repairing and expansion of existing factories is of primary importance for the economic progress of the country. Undoubtedly, the shortage of electric power in Iran at the present time is one of the major causes of a deteriorating economy and industry

5- The new kinds of energy

The new sources of energy, especially sun energy, has to be studied in Iran for prospective resources in the future. According to the opinion of experts, the basic source of energy in the future,instead of oil, would be the sun energy. Even today, in some western countries, and in many countries of Asia such as India and Israel, some part of their electric power especially for agricultural and home usage is provided by sun energy. To achieve this purpose, it is necessary to establish special institutions with adequate credit. These institutions in preparing projects for developing sun energy should exchange views with other countries like India in order to benefit from their experience in this field. Iran has an abundant amount of sunlight nearly in all areas, and the distance between towns and rural areas is very great. It would be advantageous to expand solar energy.

The conditions of Iran are not favorable to develop nuclear energy. Raw materials and technology would have to be imported from foreign countries. In addition, the country has frequent violent earthquakes regularly , that would expose the country to the dangers of atomic radiation. Undoubtedly, the Shah's ambitious program of installing twenty reactors in Iran was not in the best interest of the country. Some people believe that in order to acquire knowledge about nuclear technology, it is advisable to complete construction of the reactor in Bushihr that was 85% complete before the downfall of the Shah.

Development of transport

The development of roads and a public transport system in towns and between towns and rural areas in Iran is of great importance for economic progress, as well as for creating economic and political unity in the country.

The public transport system is more economical than every one having a private car. In addition, it prevents pollution of the environment. Consequently, instead of expanding private-car-producing industries, it is advantageous to produce more public transport vehicles as buses, railroads and etc.

In regards to the automobile industry, it is advisable to have few factories, expand them and produce only a limited number of private model cars.

The railroads of Iran are non-electric and have only one line, in the future, they should be expanded with two lines running possibly by electric power. It will require a large investment to construct secondary roads, rural roads and railroads, but it is essential for economic development.

As we pointed out in the second chapter of this book, the implementation of the law of foreign trade monopoly, before the second world war, had favorable effects on economic progress and foreign trade. The foreign trade of the country was in arrear for long periods of time - was balanced and even during the last two years before the war, it had surplus, and at the same time, capital goods needed by newly established industires were imported from foreign countries. During the second world war, and many years after that period, the above law was in practice, abandoned, and substituted by the policy of free trade followed by the government, for the purpose of combating inflation that was created in the country during war time. As a result of this policy, the import of luxury and non-essential goods flooded the domestic markets. The increase of imports did not succeed to improve inflation, it created a disequilibrium of foreign trade. The exports of the country that consisted of a few items of raw material, agricultural products and carpet, did not increase parallel to imports, and most of the imports was financed by the oil income. The deficit of foreign trade in recent years became so big that 90% of the imports was financed by the oil income. During the third and fourth plans, there had been some change in the composition of exports and imports. In regards to imports, the part of consumer goods decreased, but on the contrary, the part of capital goods increased, and for the first time, a considerable amount of industrial goods were exported.

After the revolution, because of decrease in production of agricultural and industrial products, the volume of imports of consumer goods especially food products increased sharply, and nearly the whole of the oil income was used to finance the imports of those products.

Some believe in Iran, that if foreign trade is nationalized, the public interest would be better served. But the government does not have an adequate number of qualified personnel to handle thousands of import and export items.

The following points are recommended to be considered in formulating foreign trade policy:

1- Imports of luxury and non-essential goods to be prohibited, as well as, buying and selling them in the shops, in order to prevent smuggling of those goods.

2- It is necessary to grant facilities for importation of capital goods required for industries as custom duty exemption, and so on.

3- Import of machine tools, raw material, and semi-finished goods that are produced at home to be limited to the amount equal to the shortage of supply to meet demand. The import of such goods should be subject to adequate import duties in order to protect domestic production.

4- Import duties on consumer goods that are produced at home, but their supply is not enough to meet demand, only the amount that is necessary to protect and promote internal production.

5- Production of basic industries as iron mill, and machine tool factories,to be performed at full capacity and even expanded in order to reduce the dependency of the country to foreign countries.

6- Government by appropriate ways should encourage the exports of traditional exports, as well as new products as industrial goods in order to make the country's exports more varied.

7- In commercial agreements with other countries, as well as, with economic unions like the European common market, countries should be inserted and confirmed that there would be a reasonable proportion between exports and imports of Iran with those countries. Bilateral agreements between Iran and socialist countries should be so arranged that the amount of imports and exports are always in balance.

8- The exports should be standard to the international markets and the quality of them controlled by the government so that Iran's products could compete with similar products of other countries in world markets.

9- Custom duties imposed on raw materials and semi-finished goods used for producing exports should be refunded at time of export in order that the exports of country to be able to compete in foreign markets with similar products of other countries.

10- A special organization is to be created in order to take serious action for promoting the exports of the country as marketing, export insurance, subsidizing some exports if necessary and so on.

Fiscal policy

Fiscal policy, by two ways: first, different sources of taxes, and secondly, different ways of spending it, has important effects in the economic development, and distribution of wealth and incomes in the country. In democratic countries, at the present, the fiscal policy is the most important tool at the disposal of government to provide social justice and welfare for people of the country.

In Iran, in the past, the main purpose of fiscal policy has been to provide revenues for the government, that was mostly collected through indirect taxes, and therefore, it was mostly paid by low income groups. But the rich citizens in Iran have always been able to evade the appropriate taxes. On the other hand, the main portion of government revenues were spent to construct infrastructure and public services for upper stratum of society in big cities, as establishing health services, and transport systems, etc. We can say that in the past, the taxes were paid by the poor but spent for the rich.

In the welfare state program, that we are proposing for Iran, the goal of the fiscal policy should not be only acquiring revenues for government, but its aim should be to establish economic democracy, social justice, just redistribution of wealth and incomes, and encouragement of productive activities useful for all people and also discouraging speculation on land, and other unproductive activities. For achieving this purpose, the main part of the taxes should comprise of direct taxes. Indirect taxes on essential goods should be reduced, but increased on non-essential goods.

The government's fiscal policy in the future should be: imposing progressive direct tax on wealth and income, and on the contrary, granting exemptions to low income groups and by applying this method, decrease inequality of wealth and incomes in the country, and transform the existent two societies to one city.

Regarding the government's expenditures: government should eliminate luxury and non-essential expenditures, prevent waste, and reduce bureaucracy as far as possible. It should also utilize most of its' expenditure in rural areas and small towns to eliminate all discrepancies existing between big cities, small cities and rural areas inherited from the past so that all people of the country have a reasonable standard of living in the present and in the future.

Monetary and credit policy

The monetary policy comprises of: control of the volume of money, exchange rate, credit volume and its' distribution between different sectors of the economy, fixing interest rates, encouraging savings and investments in productive activities.

The most important aims of monetary policy of the government should be to provide financial means for the development of economic and social projects, protecting the internal and external value of the national money, and prevent inflation or depression.

In order to avoid inflation, the increase of the volume of money should be moderate and proportionate to the increase of production. Allocation of credits among different sectors of the economy including agriculture, industries, services and trade and construction should be made proportionate to the importance of each sector to the economy of the country and welfare of the people.

In Iran, establishing a balance between total demand and supply of credits is not adequate for just distribution of credits, because this policy would encourage the use of credits mostly in trade and speculation in land, but productive activities would not receive sufficient credits. Consequently, the central bank of Iran should direct, and control the banking system to allocate credits to different sectors of the economy according to the requirements of projects within the framework of the general economic and social plan. For example, the banks could grant credits with low interest for construction of cheap houses and apartments for the people of low income groups and be compensated by subsidies paid to them by Central bank to the amout equal to the difference between those rates and market rates of interest.

The Iranian Central bank having the legal powers in fixing different rates of interest for different kinds of economic activities, in determining the maximum amount of credits for each kind of economic activity, is able to balance and establish equilibrium between volume of means of payment and supply of goods and services. The Central bank also has the power to prevent the flight of capital, encouraging exports and discouraging imports of non-essential goods. By pursuing this policy, harmony to the financial, trade, economic policy, and a healthy economic development in the country is achieved.

Interest rate has an important role in the economy of modern societies and is different from usury

Some fanatical religious individuals have the opinion that interest is usury and therefore, it should be prohibited.

According to the Islamic law, if an individual

lends 10 kilos of wheat to another and in due time he receives 11 kilos of wheat, the extra one kilo is usury.

Considering the above interpretation of usury, we believe that for the following reasons, interest does not coincide with usury. Furthermore, the banking system of modern societies without receiving and paying interest would not be able to perform its duty of mobilizing savings and allocating it to investments in productive activities:

1- If we suppose that, a person deposits 1000 rials in a bank, and the purchasing power of that sum of money, at that time to be 10 kilos wheat, and also if we suppose that the rate of inflation is 10%, then if at the end of the year that person instead of 1000 rials receives 1100 rials, he would not receive anything extra in addition to his own money, because the purchasing power of 1000 rials at the beginning of the year and of 1100 rials at the end of the year are the same. Therefore we can say: payment of interest to the extent that compensates deterioration of the purchasing power of money is not usury.

2- If banks receive no interest, they would not have any income, and in a short time, their capital would be used up in paying salaries of personnel and administrative expenses, and would soon go bankrupt.

3- Usually some of the bank loans are not receivable and would be considered as lost as a result of bankruptcy of borrowers, and if the banks do not receive interest, it is not certain from where they can compensate those losses.

4- If the banks do not pay interest on the savings of people, then the people would not have incentives to deposit their money in the banks and as a result, the volume of bank savings would decrease. Consequently, banks would not be able to grant credits for agricultural and industrial investments.

5- In all countries, the priority of economic activities is usually determined through interest rates. If capital is put at the disposal of individuals and business men free of interest, mostly the capital would go to unhealthy and unprofitable projects and activities, and not to profitable and healthy ones. For this reason, even in the Soviet Union, in the first years after the revolution, interest payments were prohibited, in recent years, it was established again.

Undoubtedly, the necessity of interest payments does not prevent the banks from granting loans for some social reasons with very low interest rates, allowing credits to low income groups for house building, or to peasants for buying agricultural tools.

For example, the banks may grant loans to those people at 2% rate and they themselves pay 6% interest to savings and the Central bank pays the banks 4% to compensate their losses.

Inflation and its effects

Iranian economy in the last 5 years before the revolution, was affected with galloping inflation. During the revolution, inflation intensified and now, it is more than 50% a year.

In Iran, inflation is a result of many factors, of which the most important ones are: existence of disequilibrium and disharmony between different sectors of the economy. For example, slower increases of agricultural products in comparison with industrial products or services, predominance of monopoly elements in the industrial sector, insufficiency of infrastructure as ports, and shortage of some resources as skilled workers and so on. We consider these factors as structural factors. In addition to structural factors, the great increase of volume of money and credits, vast increase of governmental expenditure with deficit financing, and raising the price of imported goods also influenced the price rise in the country.

Depression of agriculture and its low productivity has caused the continual increase of food and raw material prices. Increase of costs and profits in industries have pushed the prices of industrial products upward. Great increase of the volume of money and credits has made demand to raise more than the supply of goods and services and consequently, intensified the rise of prices.

Unfavorable effects on inflation

Inflation has many undesirable effects on the economy and social conditions of the country of which the most important are:
Inflation encourages speculation and unproductive activities, flight of capital from the country, and creates uncertainity in conditions. As a result, investment in productive activities decreases. Furthermore, rapid and continuous inflation through different changes in prices, wages, salaries in different sectors of the economy causes great changes in distribution and composition of expenditures. That usually is to the disadavantage of low income groups, and small savers. On the contrary, inflation is to the advantage of rich people and speculators, so that rich becomes richer and the poor beomes poorer.

To neutralize the disadvantageous effects of inflation on low income groups, it is necessary to compensate and rectify salaries, wages and pensions of retired persons by using the consumer index prices. On the other hand, the government should take away some portion of unearned income acquired by speculators and profiteering people by taxing them progressively in proportion to the level of their incomes.

The government can prevent inflation by way of choosing an appropriate monetary, financial and fiscal policy, and preparing development programs based on physical and human resources of the country, not only based on financial resources.

The government through choosing and implementing the right monetary and financial policy, and fair adjustment of incomes by way of imposing appropriate taxes to rich people and on non-essential goods would be able to limit production and consumption of luxury goods, and divert the financial and human resources of the country to provide goods and services needed for all citizens. We believe that the above strategy would create favorable conditions for economic development along with having stable prices.

In Iran, as the needs are unlimited, but the means to provide them are limited, the economic projects should be prepared on the basis of exact information about material, human resources and infrastructure required for carrying out those projects, both in public and private sector. The existence of only financial resources is not enough, and real physical resources adequate for implementing projects is required, otherwise rapid inflation would occur. Therefore, the government should avoid to put into action ambitious projects and even some essential but secondary projects should be postponed for later years in order to have a healthy and steady development along with stable prices.

Education and training

Education, professional training, and spread of literacy all over the country, are one of the most essential conditions for economic progress and establishment of a welfare state in the country. The most important duty of governmnet in economic and social development is to put at the disposal of all boys and girls in the country, education and training facilities. An appropriate education would create a climate that enables all citizens to become acquainted with the country's political and social issues, and to undertake their fate in their own hands. The education system of the country should transform young boys and girls of the country into men and women capable of being self-reliant, having initiative and creative powers and possessing a national and cultural consciousness.

There is no doubt that colonization and exploitation of one country by another is the result of superiority of one country over another country, from the point of view from science and technology. Backward countries are countries whose people buy capital goods and consumer products from other countries instead of producing those goods internally.

It is believed that poverty in many underdeveloped countries primarily is due to their lack of knowledge in science and moral virtues. Therefore, it would be erroneous to divide the countries of the world into rich and poor according to material possessions, but it is more correct to divide them into rich in science and moral virtues, or poor in science and moral virtues.

Today, the underdeveloped countries, if they wish to eliminate exploitation and colonization, they should equip themselves with the same weapons used by those countries who adhere to exploitation and colonization, utilizing scientific and technological powers. We have to point out that in this respect, it is of no use to organize street demonstrations and shouting slogans against imperialists and exploiters as the present government does in Iran, and at the same time, close down the universities forcing scientists, researchers and educated people to leave the country. This method of the Iranian government makes the country more dependent on foreign countries, and exposes the country to foreign exploitation and domination.

Japan, considered today as one of the most important and advanced countries in the world, has as its most dynamic resource - human resource with favorable characteristics for economic progress. 100% of the Japanese people are literate and have some kind of education. 40% of them have finished secondary schools and 20% have university degrees. In Iran, according to census performed before the revolution, 70% of the workers were illiterate, 24% have finished primary school, and 5% secondary school, and less than 1% have some kind of higher education. In recent years, before the revolution, one of the bottlenecks of the economic development was a shortage of skilled workers and specialists in agriculture and industries.

The educational program should respect the national culture, values and history of the country. In preparing the educational and training programs, we have to combine reasonable national traditions with the best and suitable ones of the world's culture. The countries that substitute national culture to foreign culture, disrupt the essence of the nation and alienate the people from themselves and their environment.

The important duty of government in respect to education, in rectifying the problem of illiteracy of all Iranians, is to establish faith in young boys and girls in the national culture, history and moral values and virtues, and annihilate unfavorable characters that are hindrances for economic and social growth.

Unfortunately, the people of Iran for some historical reason, possess some undesirable characters. If they are not changed by way of a correct education system, the country will not have real progress and democracy will not prevail. The important undesirable features of the Iranian character that should be eliminated by an appropriate educational and training system are as follows:

The undesirable features of the Iranian character

The Iranian people have many good characteristics and moral virtues, rich culture and tradition sensitive spirit, poetic talent, kindness, hospitality, and so on. But at the same time, most people because of some historical events and foreign influences have undesirable features in their characteristics that are unfavorable for economic, social progress and democracy - the most important of which are as follows:

1- The people usually prefer their personal short term interests to long term interest of society. Therefore, it is a well known saying in Iran: "Iranians are successful in individual athletic games, such as halter and wrestling, but are not good in group games as football."

2- Most people make judgement about different issues according to their sentiments and feelings and not according to logic and reason.

3- If they have good feelings about someone they admire, and speak highly of him. In fact, they consider him a saint. But if the reverse is true, they accuse him unjustly. For most Iranian people, human beings are absolute good or absolute bad.

4- The majority of the people are not ready to toleate the opinions of others who disagree with them, and consider them traitors. They try to wipe them out and make them cheap in society.

5- The sentiments of the people could be aroused and manipulated, and their feelings are easily provoked and agitated.

6- Because of historical precedents, most Iranian people believe in a leader, and if the leader is powerful and decisive they follow him unquestionably, spoil him until he becomes corrupt and turns into a dictator. If the leader is weak, they have no respect for him and consider all of his actions selfish and not in the best interest of all of the people.

7- The majority of people give only lip service to freedom, democracy and other social ideals. If their personal interest was in contact with those principles and ideals, they would give preference to their personal interests. For example, in elections, if fraud and trickery is to the benefit of their candidate, they approve, but otherwise, they criticize.

8- Most people are honest and correct in their private life and in their transactions and relations with other people, but in regards to public properties, there is vast corruption in public administration.

9- They are sensitive about the change of power, and have the tendency to change over night with an explosion of sentiments.

11- Usually, every desirable event that occurs in the country, Iranians can relate it to some foreign country. In the past, that foreign country was England, and today, it is the United States of America.

12- The Iranians have a tendency to emulate Europeans and Westerners to the point that they become more westernized and Europeanized than the Westerners and Europeans. On the other hand, they are subject to a fanatic change in an extreme manner that they condemn everything about western and European civilization.

Undoubtedly, the above mentioned characteristics are not inherent vices of the Iranian people. But on the contrary, these characteristics are being created by some undesirable historical events. It is proven that human beings inherently are alike and good, but historical situations form the character of the people in society. To create a democratic, healthy and prosperous society, it is necessary to recognize the desirable and undesirable characters of people and by a correct education system, eliminate the bad ones.

In Iran, we believe that the best way to improve the character of the people is to select virtuous, honest, dedicated and devoted individuals to government and make them a good model for the people. A proper educational system and reliable public communication would educate and train the people to be good citizens, using their leaders as guide models. India's example is a good proof of success. Ghandi, the leader of India was honest, dedicated to social issues, freedom loving, democratic and lived in very simple conditions. He and his followers set a good example for the people and the people imitated them and as a result, India has a efficient democratic government.

Professional and craft training

In Iran, a limited number of people acquire training in agriculture in comparison to other underdeveloped countries. Small number of trained people are not ready to go to rural areas and work there. They stay in the cities and are employed in other sectors of the economy.

For the development of agriculture and industries in Iran, it is important that technical colleges and schools expand their curriculum and make current revisions to suit the country's requirements. The schools and training centers should be installed in rural areas and towns, because the people should get training and employment where they live, so that they do not migrate to the big cities. All citizens, especially the peasants, should be acquainted with the benefits of knowledge and technology in practical life and have faith in their newfound awareness to solve their problems.

Scientific and research activities should be expanded

For developing the country, it is essential that research and scientific institutions have close contact and relations with industrial and agricultural firms. Although some efforts have been made in this respect by government, but it has not been sufficient. Generally, there is no connection between scientific institutions and economic activities. Consequently, the research and scientific findings have very little effect on economic development in the country.

Iran, in comparison to other developing countries, allocates small amounts of credit for research purposes. In order to have a national technology in the future and make continuous progress in the field of science and technology, it is necessary to create a favorable climate for this purpose and then allocate enough credits for research and development of sciences in Iran.

The government should specify the goals of research in different fields and communicate directly with research centers. It is urgent that the above mentioned institutions maintain a close contact, and exchange informations with each other in order to avoid duplications. Furthermore, the Iranian scientific and research institutions should establish contacts with similar institutions of other countries, because the international cooperation is advantageous for all participating countries. Also, creating favorable climates for scientific activity is essential for the progress of national technology. In the past, because of such an unfavorable climate, a considerable number of scientists and researchers left the country.

Iran also has a shortage of qualified personnel in research. This is due to a lack of facilities and encouragement, weak training systems, and students in post graduate studies who are unable to take full responsibility in research upon graduation. Furthermore, the universities should guage their studies on problems directly related to Iran's economic and social issues. Industrialists have no interest in participating in research because their technology is imported from foreign countries, and they do not feel that they are in need of domestic research.

In the future, if we wish to have domestic technology, it is urgent to encourage the universities and colleges to base their studies, with the cooperation of business firms, on the practical problems of economic development of the country, such as: quality control, design of plants, preparing technical specification, standards for products and machines, and design of new products as well as utilizing the new raw materials in production.

How to benefit from technology in economic development

One of the most important duties of Iranian researchers are to facilitate the fulfillment of the goals of economic and social development in the country. Research activity should help the country to become self-sufficient in food production, and enable it to provide the goods and services for a decent life for all.

The most important economic and social problem of the country that national technological researchers can help to solve are as follows:

1- Specifying what agricultural products in Iran's climatic conditions in different areas of the country is suitable to cultivate.

2- Recognition of the quality of soils and mineral

resources of the country.

3- Investigation of special problems in the deserts of the country and finding solutions.

4- Preparing programs for conservation and distribution of waters in the country and finding the economical methods of desaltation of sea waters.

5- How to correctly use chemical and organic fertilizers.

6- Information about the protection and conservation of agricultural products after harvest.

7- Providing technology for making simple and cheap agricultural tools in the country.

8- Improving the methods of cattle and fish breeding.

9- Providing better seeds for cultivation.

10- Information about the proper ways of using surface and underground waters and storing the waters cheaply.

11- How to manage forests and conserve them.

12- Exploiting minerals with economical and modern techniques.

13- Creating agricultural industries.

14- Research about all kinds of energy possibilities in the country.

15- Control of contageous diseases and improving the conditions of medical industries.

16- Preparing programs for family plans and population policy.

17- Information about construction of cheap and durable housing for low income groups of the country.
18- Improvement of railway systems and communication of the country.
19- Information about protection and improvement of environment.

In order to enable the universities and technical colleges to be able to perform the above research, the education and training policy should be changed. First the curriculum of the courses should be so arranged to allow extensive study on Iranian problems. Secondly, instead of sending students to foreign countries, it is advisable to provide facilities for study and research in the country. The students that study in foreign countries usually have two disadvantages in meeting Iran's requirements, first, their field of study is not appropriate, and secondly, a considerable number of them stay permanently abroad, or after coming back to Iran, after a short period, they move to other countries.

The most important fields in which the universities should have research departments are: engineering, electronics, metalorgy, design of industrial plants and machines, petrochemical, computer, and agricultural and mining industries.

Popularizing sciences and technology in Iran

One of the basic actions to expand sciences and technology in Iran is to acquaint the people with the advantages to be used in their real life and economic activites. The government should encourage the people to use their initiative and creative abilities to solve their own problems. This can be accomplished through holding seminars, and through public communications, such as radio, television, and publishing brochures and pamphlets.

The following points are recommended in order to popularize sciences and technology and the national culture:

1- Government should make an all out effort to expel illiteracy in the country.

2- In the training of young girls and boys, the educational system should advocate faith in moral values, national traditions and culture.

3- Allocation of adequate credit to research, institutions, and explicit directions to those institutions to base their studies on the problems of the country. Preparing the general lines of courses of post graduate studies in accordance with the goals of economic development of the country, and extend the capacity and improve the quality of universities and colleges so that they could be able to educate and train specialists and qualified researchers.

4- Propagiating and popularizing sciences and technology by holding seminars, through public communications, and publishing brochures and pamphlets.

5- Guaranteeing the independence of universities and colleges to be administered by the councils chosen by their own personnel.

6- Encouraging physical exercises in the country in order to improve the health of the people.

7- Encouraging the development of the national art and literature.

8- Creating a special research institution for the development of energy and also for agriculture, cattle breeding, and mining.

9- Create favorable climate for scientific activities and promote and encourage the scientists and researchers.

10- Establishment of special institutions for applying the results of researchers in industry, agriculture, mining and services.

Ownership of means of production and criterion for nationalization

There are two opposite opinions in regards to ownership of means of production: The liberal economists that are partisans of the private enterprise system, have the view that the means of production should belong to private citizens, and the government must not intervene in economic activities. They argue that private interest and social interest are always in harmony. Therefore, the individuals seeking economic activity to maximize their own profits also maximize the interests of the community. They believe that there is a social order similar to the natural order in the material world. An invisible hand makes "social interest" equal to "private interest." According to them, this invisible hand is the price system together with the existence of a perfect competition between producers and distributors of goods and services.

On the other hand, the socialist economists do not believe in the existence of such an order in society. On the contrary, they have the opinion that in free enterprise system of the economy, instead of "order", there is always "chaos". Private interest and social interest are always in the opposite direction. So when the private capitalist tries to maximize his profits, he exploits the majority of the people. Therefore, they conclude, that all means of production of a country should belong to the society.

Both of the above opinions are extreme

and neither conforms with the realities that we observe at present in the countries. First of all, there is not in existence any where a 100% private enterprise system or a 100% socialism. Nearly all countries have a kind of mixed economy, and the only difference between the countries is in the degree of public ownership and private ownership. Secondly, neither the opinion of liberal economists who claim there is always harmony between private interest and social interest, is completely correct, nor the opinion of specialists economist who believe that in all cases two kinds of interest is in disharmony is completely correct.

The third group of economists, that are called welfare economists believe that, to make a just judgment about the ownership of means of production, we have to consider the well being of the people and their ultimate goals of economic activities, and ownership of means of production as means of it's fulfillment. According to this theory, we are able to benefit from both systems. Whenever the private and social interest are in harmony and in one direction, it would be preferable that those economic activities be undertaken by the private sector, and this policy would lighten the burden of government bureaucracy. In addition, because of the existence of private initiatives and incentives, the productivity in industries, agriculture and services would rise considerably.

Therefore, the national income would be maximized. On the other hand, when the two kinds of interests are in opposite direction, it is advisable to nationalize those interests and let the government or local authorities take responsibility to perform them. Finally, when private and social interest are in one direction but are not equal, the government should by means of appropriate controls and through the system of rewards and punishments, bring the two kinds of interests to equality. We consider that this system is more appropriate for Iran. Therefore, we have made our proposal on the basis of this system.

We have to emphasize that nationalization and socialization does not mean that the economic activities are to be administered by governmental bureaucrats. In most cases, the interests of the community would be better served if the nationalized industries are run by the councils of workers and employees that are working in the nationalized firms. Undoubtedly, in order to protect the public industries, the government must control and supervise the industries being nationalized.

In most socialist countries, the main part of economic activities are administered by a vast bureaucracy without any kind of participation of workers in management and decision making. Trotsky in his exile in the year of 1930 stated: "In the Soviet Union, all means of production belongs to the government, and government in turn belongs to a few million bureaucrats." Last year, workers in Poland established a movement, called the Union of Solidarity, and they are asking from their communist government to allow them freedom to organize free unions and the right to strike, although in Western Countries many decades before, workers had acquired such rights. The Polish government refused to accept the legitimate rights of the workers, and declared martial law and began to crush the solidarity movement.

The experience of Yugoslavia in running the industry is useful for our purpose in this respect in Iran. In that country, the private enterprises that have more than 15 workers are run with participation from the council of workers. By this policy, the government succeeds in preventing the growing of bureaucracy and at the same time prevents capitalists from exploiting the workers.

The following points should be considered in regards to ownership of means of production:

1- The private ownership that is productive and creative in all fields of the economy should be encouraged. Goverment should prevent the establishment of all kinds of monopoly or oligarchy, and by appropriate means, create healthy competition among producers and distributors in order that excess profiteering and exploitation of consumers be avoided.

2- All economic activities in sectors of agriculture, industry, and services that are inherently monopolized should be nationalized and administered by government or local authorities with the participation of workers. Whenever there is some kind of monopoly or imperfect competition, the government or local authorities should control the enterprises in order to guarantee the interests of society and consumers. In business, units that employ more than 15 workers,the representative of workers should participate in administration and decision making of those enterprises.

3- The fields of economy which is disadvantageous to private activity should be determined by law and those activities, should be run by government or local authorities by participation of council workers whichever is sppropriate.

4- The government or local authorities should supervise and control the economic activities of private firms in order that the laws, regulations and the targets of the country's development plan is observed and if necessary, the government should intervene in their activities.

5- The basic and strategic industries of the country, as oil, steel, gas, electricity, water, copper, health, education, banks, insurance, infrastructure, should be nationalized and administered by government or local authorities by participation of employees and workers.

6- The forms of nationalization and regulation for indemnity payment and also participation of government, local authorities, and workers in administration of nationalized firms should be determined by proposal of the government and approval by parliment.

7- The natural resources of the country including mines, forests, seas, and rivers belong to all people. Therefore, they should be nationalized and exploited.

8- The lines of activity and limits of foreign investment should be determined by proposal of government and approval of legislative power, in order to force the international corporations and foreign capitalists to act according to the interest of the country and in conformity with the aims of economic and social development plans of the country. The government should control the activities of foreign investors so that their activities do not damage the independence of the country. The government should also in due time, make special arrangements to transfer ownership to Iranians.

9- Establishment and extension of cooperative societies of production and consumers, should be encouraged and strengthened. Regulations regarding the granting of credit facilities and tax privileges to these institutions should be determined by law.

10- In agriculture, the land should basically belong to those who cultivate it and whenever cultivation is in the form of cooperatives, it should belong to the members of cooperatives, and in the case of farm corporations, the land should belong to the farmers that are shareholders.

Workers rights

In capitalist economies, from the point of view of the employer, the work is considered as cost. From the point of view of the worker, it is considered as trouble and hardship that has to be endured in order to be able to earn income required for living. In such an economic system, a capitalist wishes that automation and repetitive work be developed as far as posible because it decreases costs and increases profits, even at the expense of creating vast unemployment.

In welfare economic systems, the aim of work is as follows:

1- Creating opportunity for all people for the purpose of developing at a full capacity the talents of all citizens.

2- Participating with others in performing common

goals, and to combat egoism and create among the workers the feeling of cooperation and mutual aid.

3- Providing necessary goods and services for the community.

In a welfare economic system, work is not only a chore, but it can be pleasure. It strengthens the mind and body of workers by reducing repetition in highly specialized work. It incorporates diversity and flexibility. It encourages workers to participate in decision making. It induces workers to like their work. As a result of oontentment of workers in this kind of welfare economy, waste would be avoided, costs lowered and cheaper, and a better quality products produced.

The Japanese experience proves the above mentioned policy. In Japan, the workers are consulted in all problems relating to production, technology and marketing. In all decisions regarding the problems of industry, advice of all who work in the plant, comprising workers, engineers, employees, employers, and directors are essential. Therefore, all workers associated in these factories are interested in the success of it and consider it their own success.

In Japan, workers seldom strike. They solve

their problems with discussion and cooperation of management. As a result of this policy, the economic success of Japan is considered a miracle, and today even the countries like the United States and European countries are not able to compete with that country in international markets. For example, in the motor car industry, previously the United States ranked first in the world. Today, Japanese competition has made the auto industry of the United States almost bankrupt.

In the year of 1981, Japan succeeded to produce 10 million cars and a considerable part of it was exported to European and American markets. Interestingly, the United States in that year produced only six million cars.

As we have pointed out earlier, the government should prevent concentration of economic and political powers in the hands of a few capitalists. In large production units where the number of workers is more than the specified number fixed by government, the workers should participate in decisions about production and distribution and other affairs of those units.

Government should support the establishment of

independent unions or workers, for the purpose of protecting the rights of workers including the right to strike.

In a welfare economy, it is the duty of the government to create opportunity of work for all. Therefore, a full employment policy should be the first goal of economic development. In addition, disguised unemployment should be included in the full employment policy of government. Presently in Iran, unemployment exceeds 4 million. There are millions of disguised unemployed who produce nothing (in government administrations and in agriculture). Recognizing unproductive jobs and surplus middlemen especially in distribution, and eliminating those jobs, is very effective in bringing down inflation and increasing the national income.

The following proposals, if enacted, would guarantee the rights of workers:

1- Every citizen has the right to work and also has the right to demand fair and satisfactory work conditions. In the welfare system, it is the duty of government to realize the above rights through preparing and carrying out appropriate economic and social programs.

2- Government should follow the full employment policy and provide unemployment benefits for those who are involuntarily unemployed. The labor law should be revised by asking advice from representatives of workers in order that their legitimate rights are observed.

3- As far as possible, the job security should be guranteed for all so that no one could be laid off for political or religious views.

4- Individuals should be free to choose employment and government must create equal opportunity of jobs for all citizens.

5- The workers associations and institutions as retirement fund, worker's banks and cooperatives societies, should be run by workers themselves with government supervision.

6- The right to strike should be recognized in labor law as the legal right of workers.

7- Government should establish health, disability, and accident insurance and retirement fund for all workers.

8- To provide facilities for workers to possess houses or flats.

9- To provide facilities for professional training of unskilled workers and retraining programs on the jobs.

10- Participation of workers in profits of firms and companies.

11- To determine minimum wage by law and revising it every year on the basis of cost of living index.

CHAPTER 18

WELFARE STATE AND DEMOCRACY

We believe that the real well being of the people is only possible in a free and democratic society and no real progress and happiness of the people is possible without having political and economic freedom that we discussed earlier in chapter 15 in detail.

Political democracy that exists in most countries is not adequate to create a welfare state because of its imperfections. Even the sociologists and experts in political sciences of those countries have criticized their political systems in recent years. They argue that only the voting of citizens of the country, once every few years, could not guarantee participation of people in government. In these countries, democracy stops at the threshold of factories and other economic institutions. But if democracy means government of people by the people for the people, then democracy should comprise participation of all people in decision making where they live, on their jobs, and where they are educated, as well as in their homes.

Unfortunately today, most societies of the world are governed from a higher fountainhead and every stratum of society endeavors to create the model that it has obtained. In these societies, it is supposed that government authorities, bureaucrats and leaders know better the interests of society than the people. Therefore, the people have to conform to their decisions. This method and course of action that is common completely in most socialist countries, and to a certain degree in western capitalist countries, is nondemocratic. Furthermore, it annihlates a variety of tastes and opinions and transforms all society to a uniformed community that is inhuman. In real democracy, every unit prepares it's own program of action and makes efforts to solve its problems with the initiative and creative power of its members. This policy is the essence and basis of self reliance, self dependence and self rule. This procedure also helps the society to be independent because a society is independent when its' people are self reliant and self dependent.

Certainly the decisions that are related to many units should be taken by upper levels, But in this case, lower levels should participate in decision making that will determine their fate. When the people participate in decision making, administering their own affairs, they become more active and work harder and better. As a result, the goals of economic and social development would be fulfilled. Furthermore, this policy,in a country like Iran,that comprises many minorities like Kurds, Balochs, Arabs, Turks and so on, creates opportunity for those minorities to administer their communities according to their own tastes and traditions, and because of their consent, the unity of nation and country would be better guaranteed.

Therefore, we can conclude, that democratic decision making in factories, governmental administrations and in education as well as transferring power of self administration and decision making in internal affairs to towns and rural areas, would attract the cooperation and participation of people in the economic, social, and political activities of the country. Consequently, real democracy and welfare states would be established in the country. Also, we can say that real democracy could be realized only by developing the councils of people in all aspects of the economy, and social problems.

Iran, unfortunately in the past centuries, has not experienced democracy and freedom. During thousands of years of absolute and despotic rule of the kings, there was no opportunity for the development of a free society, liberty, democracy, freedom and equality. People were not acquainted with the concepts of democracy, and when a parlimentary system was established in the beginning of this century, they did not make the necessary efforts to protect it.

In western societies, the people have experienced democracy for many centuries, and presently they are acquainted with the concepts of political, social and economic democracy, considering it their ideals. They are ready to make all kinds of efforts and sacrifices to protect their liberty.

In Iran, with the efforts of intellectuals, the parlimentary revolution that occurred about 75 years ago was short lived. The form of government supposed to be, so to speak, democratic. Shortly after establishment of Pahlavi dynasty, the newly attained democracy was abolished. In Iran of today, not only are the masses illiterate, but the intellectuals do not believe in a democratic society. Seldom in the country was there an election without fraud and trickery, as most people are still not ready to defend their freedom. Interestingly, if fraud in election is in favor of a group of people, they accept it and criticize it only when it is against their candidates. They do not concern themselves with the principles of free election.

As we have emphasized earlier, one of the main conditions of democracy is the tolerance to opposition. Iranian people,being very sentimental, usually are not ready to tolerate the opposite opinions and consider opposition groups as traitors, spies,or foreign elements. Under these circumstances, it is very difficult to establish democracy. In addition, democracy can develop and progress in a country where groups of people agree to some basic principles and ideals and only differ in implementation of those principles. But in Iran, the people have no such understanding. Some believe in the Islamic government on the basis of Shiet sect of Islam, which is not acceptable to Suni sect or Kurds that comprise nearly 20% of the people. Some have the opinion that the government should be separated from religion. Some believe in a republic. Others in a kingdom. Some like dictatorship of proletariat. While others prefer democracy.

In order to establish a democracy in Iran, we believe that the freedom loving and devoted people should, by all possible means, acquaint the people of their rights to freedom of participation in government. It is the duty of the government to educate the people for democracy through public communication, encouraging citizens to organize parties, and to participate in political and social affairs.

In order to guarantee the political freedom of the people, and to establish real democracy in the country, the following principles should be inserted and emphasized in the constitution of the country.

1- Freedom of expression and prevention of all kinds of censor and inquisition of opinions.
2- Freedom of press, parties, associations, workers, farmers unions, councils, and syndication.
3- Acceptance of criticism by government in all levels of government institutions.
4- Independence of judiciary power and abolition of special courts. Trials of political offenses and crimes to be performed in common courts with presence of jury elected by the people. Also the defendant's right to defend themselves, right for further appeal,

and open trials.

5- Abolition of revolutionary courts.

6- Prohibition of all kinds of torture (bodily or spiritually) and illegal imprisonment.

7- Guarantee of judicial, professional, cultural, and financial security for all citizens.

8- Equal rights for all citizens of every religion, nationality, and sex.

9- Separation of legislative, executive and judicial powers from one another and establishment of check and balance as well as harmony between them.

The Minorities rights

Granting independence to different minority groups, races and clans, for administering their own economic, social and cultural affairs in the framework of national sovereignity and unity, is one of the essential conditions to establish democracy. This policy does not conflict with the sovereignty of the country and strengthens it. Because this policy would secure the contentment of minorities and encourage them to participate willingly in development and progress, making the culture and traditions of the country more rich and varied.

The decentralized system and its advantages

In dictatorial governments (socialist or capitalist), most affairs are concentrated in the "centers" and nearly all important decisions are reached there. Provinces and towns of those societies, with no power in decision making, do not feel responsible for the progress of the respective areas. The work is performed very slowly, and usually the people become very discontent. But in a real democracy, every province, town and unit has the power to act and participate collectively. Therefore, the decision is taken rapidly and the work performed on a timely schedule.

In Iran, decentralization and granting power to local authorities is essential for the establishment of a welfare and a democratic state because distance between towns and provinces is very large. The country is comprised of different races and creed,each having a different taste, tradition and culture. Their needs are different, making it impossible for the government to comply with.

Separation between religion and politics

There is no doubt that the moral perception

all religions forbid crime, theft, lying, and so on. In this respect, the laws and regulations relating to economic, political, and social problems of the society, the right of different groups and individuals as well as the relation of one country with another -- is not the issue that religion could or should interfere with. Important religions of the past could not forsee all the technical, and social changes that occurred during the last three centuries. There is no choice for the people but to administer their economic and social affairs reasonably, logically, scientifically, by using only the moral and spiritual teachings of religion.

Today in most countries, especially in industrially advanced societies, the sphere of activity of religion is limited to the moral and spiritual aspects of human life. Government and affairs of the state is within the sphere of activity of experts, chosen by the people for this purpose. Consequently, we can conclude that religion in a welfare state should be separated from politics.

Economic democracy

As we pointed out in previous chapters, political democracy without having economic democracy has no real meaning. The individual that is hungry with no place to sleep, sick and illiterate, is neither to think freely, nor is he able to live freely and enjoy political freedom.

Economic democracy requires that in any country, all people have equal opportunity to develop all their abilities and enjoy a good life.

The following conditions are required for establishment of an economic democracy:

1- Providing an income through a full employment policy for all people that are ready to work and produce for the benefit of the society. Also, guaranteeing a minimum standard of living for those who are unvoluntarily unemployed.

2- Providing habitation for all. It is essential that re-payment of loans or rent to be of a reasonable proportion to the family income.

3- Free health service for all people with acceptable standards.

4- Free education during the first nine years of schooling for all citizens - creating technical and professional training facilities for all.

5- Providing retirement insurance for all people and pensions for the families of deceased persons. Establishment of social security for all citizens. Accident and disability insurance also is required.

6- The financial resources of the country should be allocated according to the population and real needs of provinces, towns, and rural areas. The public services and infrastructure expenditures should be fair and justly distributed among the social groups and geographical areas in order that the dualism economy and society be transformed to a single unified society.

7- The economic authorities of government responsible for preparing the statistics of growth and economic progress, should not only publish the real growth of each economic sector separately, but also determine clearly what groups and how much each group prospers from the growth. By this method, the statistics would show what has been the effect of economic development in closing the gap between the rich and the poor. In a welfare state, it is essential that there exists a reasonable proportion between "high wealth and incomes" and "low incomes and wealth."

8- Just and equal distribution of incomes and wealth should be accomblished by:

a. Imposing progressive taxes to unearned income, high income and excessive wealth as well as inheritance.

b. Real land reform.

c. Nationalization of all natural resources and also nationalization of land in big cities.

9- Lowering of indirect taxes on essential goods required for the majority of people and increase taxes on non-essential goods in order to free the resources from producing or importing non-essential goods.

10- Providing cheap habitation for low income groups such as workers and government employees.

11- Protection of consumer's interest through control of prices and qualities of products. Also elimination of excess middleman in distribution sectors.

12- Modernization of villages and small towns with the help of residents.

13- Preventing all kinds of monopolization and creating healthy competition among producers and distributors.

14- Providing an adequate public transport service in towns and in rural areas.

15- Supporting and encouraging cooperative producers and consumer societies in order to stabilize prices and fight inflation.

16- Combating inflation by carrying out an appropriate monetary, fiscal, financial and budgetary policy. In order to prevent a negative effect of inflation in the country, it is necessary to compensate the purchasing power of low income groups and retired men by indexing.